*To Ryan + Harper
on their Wedding Day
October 4, 2025
Grampa + Nena*

BUILDING A GODLY HOME

"Let us hear the conclusion of the whole matter: Fear God, and keep His commandments: for this is the whole duty of man."
Ecclesiastes 12:13

BUILDING A
GODLY HOME

NEALE PRYOR

RESOURCE
PUBLICATIONS
2205 Benton
Searcy, AR 72143

Copyright © 2022
Resource Publications

ISBN-13: 978-0-945441-71-7

Scripture taken from the NEW AMERICAN STANDARD BIBLE®, © Copyright 1960, 1962, 1963, 1968, 1971, 1972, 1973, 1975, 1977, 1995 by The Lockman Foundation. Used by permission. (www.Lockman.org)

Contents

For the Young

1. Because You Are Young — *1*
2. Do Your Parents Care? — *17*
3. Ten Commandments for Youth #1 — *31*
4. Ten Commandments for Youth #2 — *45*
5. So You Want to Get Married — *63*

For Marriage

6. Happily Ever After — *83*
7. God's Plan for Marriage — *89*
8. The Two Shall Become One — *97*

For the Home

9. Five Suggestions for Parents — *109*
10. Five More Suggestions for Parents — *117*
11. A Tribute to Christian Fathers — *125*
12. A Tribute to Christian Mothers — *135*
13. Trust in the Home — *143*
14. Forgiveness in the Home — *153*

Bibliography — *165*

Foreword

Among the churches of Christ, the name Neale Pryor has become a household name. During the time he taught Bible classes at Harding University, he was the most popular teacher on the campus. In fact, those who sat in the classes of this godly man often labeled him as one of "the greatest teachers on earth." When it was announced that Neale would not be able to teach his Sunday morning auditorium class anymore because of health reasons, both women and men wept.

As he matured as a teacher, he also matured into one of the finest preachers. For a decade or so, he and Jimmy Allen held the spring and fall meetings for the College church. Although they were opposites in delivery style, both were extremely effective in presenting the gospel to thousands of college students and people of the community. Often these meetings would have dozens of baptisms and restorations. No one grew tired of hearing these wonderful preachers deliver their sermons. If someone made a list of the great preachers of the 1980s and 1990s, Neale Pryor and Jimmy Allen would be listed among them.

Those who knew Neale well regarded him not only as a superb teacher and preacher, but they also knew him to be one the finest Christian men they had been privileged to know. He was highly educated, but he was also humble and gentle. He was as serious as teachers come; but he was happy, humorous, and easy to follow. He quickly became a friend to everyone he met; and, with his amazing memory, he would recall the names of those he met ten years after meeting them.

When God brought Neale on the world's platform of service, he gave him a great responsibility; but Neale took that challenge by the horns and gave it his best. God gave him an opportunity to change the world; and Neale Pryor, with God's grace and help, did. When he left this world in 2011, it was a much better place. He was not faultless; but, like Noah, he was "righteous, blameless in his time," and a man who walked with God (Genesis 6:9).

He has left this collection of his presentations behind, and we must read them carefully. We must listen to his words and look thoughtfully at his spirit and allow them to point us to Jesus. If we do not have Christian homes, may this book help each of us to build one.

Eddie Cloer
Professor Emeritus
Harding University

1
Because You Are Young

Let no one look down on your youthfulness, but rather in speech, conduct, love, faith and purity, show yourself an example of those who believe (1 Timothy 4:12).

What a privilege it is to be young! With your whole life before you, youth is an exciting time, isn't it? George Bernard Shaw once said that youth is such a wonderful thing that it is a shame it has to be wasted on young people.

Because you are young, you are a very important part of the world and the church right now. It may seem that older people are making much out of what you will be someday. You will be something great someday, but you are something great right now too. You are the inspiration and the hope of many.

Young people are the leaders of tomorrow. Certain work in the church can only be done by young people. If the young do not do it, it will not be done. Sometimes you may get the impression that older people are saying to you, "Just sit right there and be still. When you are thirty, we may call on you." Nothing could be further from the truth. We need you now. You are important right now!

Because you are young, you will be of even greater importance to the Lord's kingdom in years to come. You will be facing trials and overcoming problems that the older generations never faced and never attempted to solve. Because you are young, much is demanded of you, and even more will be demanded of you in the days to come. In order for you to meet these challenges, you will need three things: a faith to live by, a self to live with, and a purpose to live for.

A Faith to Live By

Nothing can be more important than a strong foundation. Your ability to endure and be successful depends upon your foundation. The deeper your foundation is the higher you can build. The huge skyscrapers in New York City are possible because they have a deep, solid foundation in underground rock.

Harding University was having a building constructed; and, for the first several months, it looked as if the workers were doing nothing. In fact, it seemed so strange that an announcement was made in chapel about it. The workers had discovered bedrock many feet below the ground level, and they were digging down to the rock and laying concrete piers for a foundation. That building will probably be around long after many others are gone because of its foundation.

In the parable of the two builders, Jesus contrasted the man who laid the foundation of his house on the sand with the man who laid his foundation on the rock. In Luke's account, Jesus pointed out the extent to which the builder went in laying this foundation: He "dug deep and laid a foundation on the rock . . ." (Luke 6:48). When the rains came and the winds blew and beat against it, it did not fall; for it was founded on the rock. Of course, the house on the sand fell. Maybe the house was just as good, but it was laid upon a poor foundation. How important it is for us to build the only lives we will ever have upon the right foundation!

In the parable of the sower, Jesus told of some seed that fell upon stony ground. Some may think of this as ground that has huge rocks in it, but it is ground that has a thin layer of topsoil over a layer of rock. The little plants wither and die because they have no depth. Lives without depth cannot last.

These illustrations emphasize the importance of a deep and abiding foundation.

Lives must have a solid foundation if they are to endure and produce fruit. That solid foundation is your faith. Because you are young, it is time for you to find the faith you will live by. On what will you base your life? What in this world is worth giving your all? By what standards will you live? What goals in life are worth striving to achieve? These are choices that only you can make. No one can, or should, make such decisions for you.

Often, parents will ask me what has happened to their teenage children. The children were faithful to attend church services and do all of the right things until they were about sixteen years of age. Then they seemed to lose all interest in the church.

Such children did not suddenly become sour at sixteen. When they were younger, the children were living according to the faith of their parents. Then the time arrived when they needed to stand on their own faith, and they had not developed any. We cannot live all of our lives on our parents' faith. God does not have any grandchildren. We may inherit our parents' physical build, brown eyes, blond hair; but we cannot inherit their faith. That is something that we must develop for ourselves.

When I was a little fellow, I believed in Santa Claus. I believed in him because my mother and father talked about Santa Claus. When I got presents on Christmas morning, it would have been foolish to question any further! As I grew older, I began to ask myself if there really was a Santa Claus. The fact that Mother and Daddy spoke of him was not enough. I needed to find out for myself.

Also, when I was very young, I believed in God. I believed in Him because my parents told me about Him. The preacher and my Sunday school teacher said that there is a God in heaven. Again, when I got older, that was not enough. I needed to find for myself reasons to believe in God.

A person who has seriously questioned his or her faith and found reasons to believe has a much healthier faith than someone who has never tried to find any answers. Because you are young, you need to ask for yourself if you should believe in God and if you should accept the Bible as God's Word.

Remember the words of the Samaritan people to the woman: "It is no longer because of what you said that we believe, for we have heard for ourselves and know that this One is indeed the Savior of the world" (John 4:42). Do not be afraid to search for the truth. Do not be afraid to probe into your faith for reasons to believe. If what you believe is the truth, then the more you investigate, the more it will shine forth. I would not want to have a faith that I feared to investigate. Too much of the right learning cannot hurt anyone.

I have had students come into my office looking rather embarrassed. They ask me timidly, "Please don't get upset with me, but how can I really know that there is a God? How can I know for sure that the Bible is God's Word?" Usually, I reply, "Well, I am glad that you are finally asking. It is wonderful that you are seeking out these answers for yourself." Everyone must go through this struggle for himself.

Christianity is a personal relationship with Jesus. Each one must find God himself. A secondhand faith is not worth much. Because you are young, you need to find Christ for yourself. You need to be convinced in your own mind of the truth of His revelation. I cannot believe for you any more than I can obey for you.

Christianity is a lonely thing. Most of serving the Lord is an individual endeavor. You have to face your own temptations. You have to obey for yourself. You will have to die by yourself. You will stand in judgment by yourself. You must believe for yourself. A faith that is internalized and personalized is one that will endure.

We have many reasons to believe in God. The creation itself is one of the greatest. Often, when I ask myself, "How can I really know there is a God and a purpose to my existence?" I look around me. Only God could make such a beautiful world. Look at the sun, moon, and stars. Look at the green grass, blue skies, and flowers around you.

Consider the delicate balances of nature: the right temperatures, the right supply of oxygen and carbon dioxide. Look at the marvel of the human body. Not even the greatest minds of our day can understand all of the processes going on inside of you. If scientists ever create life in a laboratory, it will not be an accident. It will be the result of years of research and study. Even if they produce a simple living organism, they will be far from creating a human body.

The psalmist long ago expressed these same sentiments when he said, "I am fearfully and wonderfully made" (Psalm 139:14). We read, "The heavens are telling of the glory of God; and their expanse is declaring the work of His hands" (Psalm 19:1). The heavens do not have to keep saying, "God made me! God made me!" Their very existence is sufficient to show evidence of their Creator.

Note Psalm 19:3: "There is no speech, nor are there words; their voice is not heard," yet "their line has gone out through all the earth" (19:4a). Paul said that the Gentiles should have known of God through His creation:

> For since the creation of the world His invisible attributes, His eternal power and divine nature, have been clearly seen, being understood through what has been made, so that they are without excuse (Romans 1:20).

Evidence of God's existence is all around us; we simply must open our eyes and look.

Some have the opinion that it is unscientific to believe in God, but it is more reasonable to believe in God than not to believe in Him. Is it not easier to believe in a Creator who made the worlds than to believe that all of this is the result of chance?

It takes a greater "leap of faith" to believe that matter always was and that all of this great universe just happened than it does to believe that an all-powerful and all-wise God made the worlds. You see, Christians are not the only ones who have a faith. Everyone has a faith: a faith that there is a God or a faith that there is not a God.

In a manner of speaking, we are detectives in this world, looking for clues about life. When a detective investigates a crime, he puts forth certain possible solutions. Then he asks which possibility is most likely, which solution has the fewest problems.

As we search, we ask which alternative to the origin of the universe is the most likely, which solution presents the fewest problems. The answer in the Bible is the most reasonable: "In the beginning God created the heavens and the earth" (Genesis 1:1). Plenty of evidence is available to help you find a faith to live by.

A Self to Live With

Because you are young, you need a self to live with. You will have to live with yourself for the next fifty, sixty, or seventy years. You need to spend that time with someone you like.

Some people don't like themselves. They are miserable. They take trips seeking happiness, but they are just as miserable elsewhere as they were at home. Do you know why? Because they take the source of their misery with them: It is themselves.

We should love ourselves. The Bible teaches self-love. Self-love is not the same thing as conceit. Most conceited persons really don't have much genuine self-love; they are quite insecure and have low opinions of themselves. That is why they put up the front of conceit. A person who really feels good about himself is open to others; he or she does not try to make others feel inferior. Really, self-love is the opposite of conceit.

Jesus commanded self-love. He told us to love our neighbors as ourselves (Matthew 22:39). That isn't saying much for our neighbors if we don't care for ourselves, is it? Paul encouraged husbands to love their wives by saying, "He who loves his own wife loves himself" (Ephesians 5:28b). Each one of us is worth something; we are worth loving. God made us; that gives us value. One person put it this way: "I am worth something because God made me, and God doesn't make junk!"

In order to have a self to live with, there are at least three things we need to do. *First, we need to avoid having a life filled with bitter memories and regrets.* Too many older people have regrets that haunt them in their latter years. Some would give anything to relive their days and avoid the painful mistakes they made in their youth.

Paul is an example of this. How do you suppose he felt when he went to worship with the church at Jerusalem and saw little children whose parents he had killed? Perhaps, as he spoke to some widow, he remembered the day he beat her husband to death. It would be hard to live with that, wouldn't it? It seems that Paul never completely got over what he did in his past. About twenty years after his conversion, he said, "For I am the least of the apostles, and not fit to be called an apostle, because I persecuted the church of God" (1 Corinthians 15:9).

Paul, like any other Christian, was forgiven of the guilt of his sins. Still, the memory and consequences of these mistakes stayed with him throughout his life. At times, this great man must have wept over his past life; he had done everything possible to erase those terrible crimes. Nevertheless, what was done was done; nothing could really erase what had happened in his past.

We should not wallow in self-pity over our mistakes. We cannot just lie down and do nothing the rest of our lives because of our terrible guilt. We must realize that the blood of Jesus can wash away any sin. We have to pick up the pieces and go on. Remember what Paul said: "Forgetting what lies behind and reaching forward to what lies ahead, I press on..." (Philippians 3:13, 14).

Because you are young, you don't have many bitter memories yet. It is far better never to make these mistakes than it is to try to undo what has already been done. Resolve to keep your life free of these regrets. We may pull a nail out of a board, but the scar remains. Keep your past from being scarred. Don't do things now that you will regret the rest of your life.

This is particularly true in the area of boy-and-girl relationships. Many young men and women have deep regrets and often emotional scars because of intimacy before marriage. I have talked with many about this. I recall girls wanting to know if they can ever get married after what they have done. I remember one girl screaming, "I hate him! I hate him!" Of course, she was a willing partner and was as much to blame as he was. I wanted to reach back in the past and pull out that mistake; but I couldn't, and neither could anyone else.

What has been done may be forgiven; you can thank the blood of Jesus for that. Still, the memories and regrets, and often the consequences, of sexual impurity haunt people for the rest of their lives. This problem is not restricted to girls alone. Boys have just as much of a need to keep themselves pure as girls do.

Very few young people who have engaged in sexual intimacy before marriage will live without regret. It is difficult to find an older person who would not recommend waiting until marriage for such intimacy. I can almost guarantee that, if you give in to such temptation, you will one day regret your actions. At the moment, it may not seem like such a big problem; but you are creating memories that will remain for your entire life. You are doing something that you will later wish you could erase from your past.

Boys, for the sake of the girl you are with, for the sake of your parents and for hers, for the sake of the girl you will marry one day, for the sake of the boy she will marry one day, for the children you will have, for the children she will have—keep yourself pure. What you are doing affects far more than just the two of you.

Hardly anything will enhance your wedding day more than the clear conscience that you are a virgin. Perhaps nothing is more delightful for a honeymoon than the purity of the two people who are being united. One of the most important gifts you can give to your future spouse is a pure conscience and a clean past.

Second, to have a self to live with, you need to accept yourself as you are. Very few of us are just what we want to be. Some wish they were taller; some wish they were shorter. Some want to be heavier; some, thinner. Some want to have straight hair; some want curly hair. Some would just be happy to have hair! No one is exactly like he or she wants to be. We have to make the best of what we have.

When God made us, He did not ask us how we wanted to look. We might have suggested several changes. Still, we must learn to accept what we have been given and make the best of it.

Paul wished that he did not have a thorn in the flesh. No one knows what this thorn in the flesh was. It may have been poor eyesight; it could have been a number of other things. It does seem to have been some physical problem or shortcoming. Paul prayed to the Lord to remove it. God answered his prayer—not by removing it, but by giving him the strength to bear it. He had to learn to accept it (2 Corinthians 12:7–10).

In the Sermon on the Mount, Jesus told His disciples to learn to accept what they could not change. He asked them, "And who of you by being worried can add a single hour to his life?" (Matthew 6:27). In other words, can you make yourself live any longer by worrying about it? A reading of this verse in the King James Version says, "Which of you by taking thought can add one cubit unto his stature?" A cubit is supposed to be the length from the elbow to the tip of the middle finger, eighteen inches. Measure yourself, and see if your forearm is eighteen inches. If not, should you worry about it? Do you suppose that worrying could make you grow a few inches taller? How foolish it is to waste our time and energy worrying over what cannot be helped.

We have two alternatives. We can fret over our shortcomings and make ourselves and everyone around us miserable, or we can accept ourselves for what we are and go ahead with the business of living. We need to follow the words of a familiar prayer: "God, grant me the serenity to accept the things I cannot change."

Really, the things that are so important to teenagers, such as looks and physique, are not all that important in later years. It is of the utmost importance to young girls to be attractive in order to find a good husband. To young men, it is of the greatest importance to be physically desirable, to be athletic, so they can impress the girls. Physical beauty is important to us. Peter advised women,

> Your adornment must not be merely external—braiding the hair, and wearing gold jewelry, or putting on dresses; but let it be the hidden person of the heart, with the imperishable quality of a gentle and quiet spirit, which is precious in the sight of God (1 Peter 3:3, 4).

Many of us will never win acclaim over our outward appearance, but we can all develop inward beauty. Inward beauty not only outlasts the outward, but it also outshines it. If you are not successful in life, it will not be because of what is on the outside; it will be because of what is on the inside. That is the beauty of the soul, a beauty within the reach of every one of us.

Third, in order to have a self to live with, you need to find what you can do in life and do it to the best of your ability. Many people are miserable because they are trying to be what they are not. As Christians, we are all members of one body. The members of the body should not, and do not, try to do the same thing. Can you imagine the frustration of trying to hear with an eye or to see with an ear? What part of the body are you? If you are an eye, then get busy seeing. Maybe you are meant for a less noticeable position, like an intestine or a part of the liver. These parts are just as important.

Take pride in what you are doing. We can feel good about ourselves when we are doing well that which we have the talent to do. Be the best that you can be. One of the greatest compliments ever paid to Jesus was the one spoken by outsiders after He had healed a deaf mute. They said of Him, "He has done all things well" (Mark 7:37). Can that same thing be said of you?

Many times, you can get by with less than your best. However, you owe it to yourself, even if to no one else, to give everything your best. You know when you have given your all. Nothing gives more satisfaction than a job well done. That is one further step in developing a self to live with. No one else in the world is quite like you. You should not ever try to be anyone else.

Others may have qualities that you would like to copy in your life, but you should be proud of the unique qualities that make you who you are. If you try to be an imitation of someone else, you will never be anything more than an imitation. Be the real thing: Be you. God has endowed you with a certain combination of talents and qualities that no one else will ever have. Don't fret because you are not someone else. Be yourself, and be proud of yourself.

A Purpose to Live For

Ask yourself this question: "Why are we all here?" To find the answer, you must ask three other questions: "Where did I come from?"; "What am I doing here?"; "Where am I going?" Some would have you to believe that you came from lower forms of life through a process of evolution, that you are on this earth taking up space and using up commodities, and that you are going back to the dust from which you came.

The Bible teaches that you came from the hand of God, that you are on this earth to serve your Maker and fellow man, and that you will eventually go into one of two vast eternities. If the second set of answers is true, it makes a great difference as to your purpose in life. If the first set of answers is true, then it doesn't matter much. God is telling you that it does matter!

Because you are young, you need to have the right purpose in life. Right now, it is more important what direction you are headed than where you are on the road. Your direction today will determine your destination forty or fifty years from now—or a billion years from now.

It is easy to get distracted from the important by the urgent. Often, the things nearest to us look the largest. If you put your hand in front of your eye, that hand appears to be larger than the whole world. Similarly, pressures of the moment are often blown entirely out of proportion, while long-range goals, though more important by far, seem less important.

Too many seem to be suffering from spiritual myopia. "Myopia" is nearsightedness; the nearsighted person can see clearly what is close to him, but he cannot see what is in the distance. His whole world is the few feet around him. Glasses and contact lenses can correct this problem physically, but spiritual nearsightedness is often much harder to remedy. Peter spoke of such. After listing the Christian graces, or virtues, he said, "For he who lacks these qualities is blind or short-sighted, having forgotten his purification . . ." (2 Peter 1:9).

Some people at Harding University have used the expression "majoring in minors." College students often focus on minor activities—athletic and social events. When they receive their grades, they see that they have not been giving attention to the more important aspects of earning an education.

In Philippians 1:10, Paul prayed that the brethren might "approve the things that are excellent." Literally, this means to "distinguish the things that differ." In other words, we must separate the important from the less important. To put it another way, we need to major in majors.

According to Paul's thinking, life has only one major purpose. He said, "For it is for this we labor and strive, because we have fixed our hope on the living God . . ." (1 Timothy 4:10). Paul was a specialist. We live in an age of specialization. In many areas of life, we see the value of specialization. We have to specialize if we are to achieve excellence. We cannot be and do everything. Paul summed up his purpose with the words ". . . but one thing I do . . ." (Philippians 3:13). Paul did many things in life, but they all were centered on the one purpose of serving God.

You are a Christian by profession. Whatever else you do should be determined by your commitment to Christ. This one thing should determine your lifetime work, your choice of friends and associates, your hobbies and recreation, your choice of a husband or wife. We are soldiers of Christ. "No soldier in active service entangles himself in the affairs of everyday life . . ." (2 Timothy 2:4). What would you think of a soldier who was so busy with his hobby that he did not have time to go to battle? We are soldiers of Christ first, and anything else comes second.

To me, it seems that the most important text in the entire New Testament is Matthew 16:26. If I could burn in the minds and hearts of young people one idea, that would be it. It puts life in perspective. In that verse, Jesus asked,

> For what will it profit a man if he gains the whole world and forfeits his soul? Or what will a man give in exchange for his soul? (Matthew 16:26).

If you reach every goal you set in life but lose your soul, you are a miserable failure. I hope that you get the education you want, that you find the husband or wife you seek, and that you achieve your greatest dream. Remember, though, if you lose your soul, it would be better for you if you had never been born. If that happens, when you stand before the judgment, you will wish that you had never been born!

A young man was telling his father about his plans for the future. He had selected his college and had already decided on his major. His father asked him, "What then?" He replied that he would get a good job and be a success in his chosen field of endeavor. His father asked again, "What then?" He said that he planned to get married and have a good family with three or four children. His father asked again, "And what then?"

The son had not anticipated that many "What then?" questions. He said, "Well, I guess I will get old. Everyone else does." His father persisted, "And what then?" He said, "I guess some day I will die. Everyone else does." Once more, his father asked, "And what then?" Have you ever given thought to that final question? When this world is no more, when the Lord has come to claim His own, when the last battle has been fought and the last dollar earned—"What then?"

Conclusion

It is great to be young. May God bless you. While you are still in your youth, perhaps even today, may you find these three essentials: a faith to live by, a self to live with, and a purpose to live for.

QUESTIONS

1. What three things do young people need in order to face the challenges of life?

2. What is the solid foundation needed for a life to endure and produce good fruit?

3. What three basic questions must be answered in life?

4. What was Paul's major purpose in life?

5. Why is Matthew 16:26 considered to be one of the most important verses in the New Testament?

2
Do Your Parents Care?

He who withholds his rod hates his son,
But he who loves him disciplines him diligently
(Proverbs 13:24).

Yes, Parents Care

In Genesis 22, the Word of God tells us that God spoke to Abraham. He told him to arise and take his son, his only son Isaac, whom he loved, to make a sacrifice in the land of Moriah (22:2). The phrasing seems as though God must have wanted to emphasize how special Isaac was. Very early the next day, Abraham sat on his donkey and set out with Isaac and some servants to whatever place God had told him. On the third day, they reached that place. Abraham left the servants at the foot of the hill. He told them, "Stay here with the donkey, and I and the lad will go over there; and we will worship and return to you" (Genesis 22:5).

I imagine that, as Abraham and Isaac went up the hill together, it was a very quiet trip. I know there was so much on the heart of Abraham that very little could have been on his lips. In 22:7, Isaac perhaps interrupted the silence when he said to Abraham, "My father!" Abraham said, "Here I am, my son" (22:7a). Continuing in 22:7b, Isaac said, "Behold, the fire and the wood, but where is the lamb for the burnt offering?" In reply, "Abraham said, 'God will provide for Himself the lamb for the burnt offering, my son.' So the two of them walked on together" (22:8).

When they came to the place, Abraham tied his son on the altar. He drew back a knife and was about to kill Isaac, but God from heaven stopped his hand. He said,

> Abraham, Abraham! . . . Do not stretch out your hand against the lad, and do nothing to him; for now I know that you fear God, since you have not withheld your son, your only son, from Me (22:11, 12).

What gives the story the impact it carries is the fact that this father loved his son.

In 2 Samuel 21, we find a less familiar story about Rizpah, a wife of Saul. Saul had killed some of the Gibeonites; and, out of vengeance, the Gibeonites had slain some of the sons of Saul. Two sons of Rizpah were slain and left unburied. Rizpah, from the beginning of harvest, which would be early spring, stayed with the corpses until the beginning of the rain, which would have been in the fall. She permitted neither the birds nor the beasts of the field to harm the lifeless forms of her two sons. When David heard of this, he gave her sons a royal burial. This mother loved her sons.

In 2 Kings 4, we read about a very hospitable Shunammite woman. She always provided food and shelter for Elisha when he was in that area. She even built a room for the prophet. Out of gratitude, Elisha promised her that God would give her a son, and He did. When the child was old enough, he was out in the fields with the reapers and his father one day, when he suddenly cried out, "My head! My head!" The father called the servants and told them to take the lad to his mother. The mother held that little boy on her knees until he died. He died in the lap of his mother.

She took the lifeless form of her child and laid it on Elisha's bed. Then she saddled her donkey and rode as fast as she could toward Mount Carmel, fifteen or twenty miles away, to find

Elisha. Elisha's servant ran to meet her and asked if all was well with her, with the child, and with her husband. She said, "It is well" (4:26); but when she reached Elisha, she fell at his feet and grabbed onto him. His servant tried to pull her away, but Elisha said to leave her alone because she was in great agony. The Lord had not made him aware of what had happened. She told of the death of her son. Elisha went to the boy and stretched himself upon the child. With the help of the Father in heaven, he restored that child's life. The woman of Shunem was another mother who loved her son.

In Matthew 15 and Mark 7, we read of a woman who approached Jesus. She was a Syrophoenician woman, a Gentile. She begged Jesus to help her because her child was afflicted with a demon. She did not say, "Have mercy on my daughter"; she said, "Have mercy on me." She identified that closely with her little girl. Our Lord did not even answer her. He ignored her completely. I might have gotten angry and left, but this woman had no pride where the welfare of her daughter was concerned.

She continued to ask Jesus for help, and the disciples said to Him, "Send her away, because she keeps shouting at us" (Matthew 15:23). Jesus said, "I was sent only to the lost sheep of the house of Israel" (15:24). She persisted: "Lord, help me!" (15:25). Then our Lord insulted her: He said, "It is not good to take the children's bread and throw it to the dogs" (15:26). This woman humbly said in 15:27, "Yes, Lord; but even the dogs feed on the crumbs which fall from their masters' table." The Lord blessed that woman and healed her daughter. Again, we see a mother who loved her child.

Not too long after that, on the hill of Calvary, on a Friday at three in the afternoon, the Son of God was hanging on a cross. When blood was streaming from the wounds and forming pools on the ground below, as He felt the very essence of life ebbing from Him, He pierced the darkness with a cry: "Eli, Eli, lama sabachthani?" That means "My God, My God, why have You forsaken Me?" (Matthew 27:46). The heart of the

Father in heaven must have been wrung by His cry. How difficult it must have been for God—even with His divine, superhuman strength—to turn His back and leave His Son there to die! The Father in heaven loved His Son.

Really, I just have one point I want to get across to you. Your family cares about you. I do not know why we parents care so much about our children. I do not know why we love you when you get in trouble, make messes, break things, cost so much to take care of, put dents in the cars, and eat up all the groceries—but we do love you. Maybe it is because you are a part of us. You carry our name, and sometimes we look at you in horror as we notice you beginning to look like us. We realize that you are us, in a sense.

After we are gone, the one claim to immortality on this earth we will have is that you will live on. Maybe it is instinct. Even dumb animals take care of their own. I remember one time, when I was a little fellow at my aunt's farm, helping myself to one of the baby chickens. The hen apparently wanted it worse than I did, so I let her have the thing. One chicken was not worth all I was about to go through to get it. I threw it right back down.

In 1 Kings 3, two harlots took their problem to Solomon. One of them said that each had borne a child, but one had lain on her child and had killed it. She claimed that the other mother had swapped the two babies, taking the living child and leaving her the dead one. The second mother said that the living one was hers and insisted, "The dead one is your son" (3:22). Solomon said to bring a sword so they could divide the living child in half, since each mother said the child was hers. The real mother cried out, "Oh, my lord, give her the living child, and by no means kill him" (3:26). When the other woman said to divide him, Solomon could see who the real mother was.

Maybe we parents love you children because we have so much invested in you. We brought you into this world; we fed you; we worked with you; we have tried to mold your lives.

DO YOUR PARENTS CARE?

We have spent time, money, and effort on you. You are what we have built. Anything we invest that much time and effort in is very near and dear to us. Maybe that is why we love you. Maybe we love you because you need us. Everybody needs to be needed. It is wonderful to have someone who needs you. How wonderful it is to have you children need us! It is sad when we one day learn that you don't need us as you once did.

As I was preparing this lesson, I asked some young people how they knew that their parents loved them. I asked what their parents do that shows their love. I have before me an unedited list.

This is exactly the way they told it:

"They tell me 'no.'"
"They spank me when I need it."
"They feed me."
"They provide for my needs."
"They send me to a good school."
"They read to me when I am scared."
"They sang to me and rocked me when I was little."
"They console me when I am down."
"They spend time with me and play with me, even when there are other things they need to be doing."
"They hunt jobs for me."
"They help me when I get into trouble."
"They give me privileges and responsibilities and take them away if they see the need."
"They take care of me when I am sick."
"They are concerned with who my friends are."
"They set a good example before me."
"They let me learn and do for myself."
"They are concerned about how I dress and look, and whether or not I get a haircut."
"They act like a friend toward me."
"They tell me they love me."
"Sometimes they try to kiss on me."

Not every parent is an expert in all of these areas. Some are better at some than at others.

My mother said that I always wanted my father in preference to her, except for when I got sick. I had no use for my father when I got sick. He was not a good caretaker. One time, I ran to him, hurt and crying. I do not know what I had done. He looked at the damage, and he said, "Well, it will feel better when it quits hurting." That is not what a fellow needs. He needs a mother to kiss it and be sympathetic and do something about it.

Sometimes, when I was about ten, I could not go to sleep. I would call out to my parents that I could not go to sleep. Mother would come in and pat me once or twice, and that was all it usually took. She must have been really tired one night because she sent my father in. That was a mistake. He came in and lay down beside me, reached over, and patted me twice. Then he was snoring. He was sound asleep.

He was the only man I ever knew who could go to sleep and then lie down. I called out and said, "Mama, Daddy is snoring and keeping me awake." The next morning, I fussed at him about that. I told him that he was not much help. He said, "Well, I don't know what you are complaining about. I lay down right beside you and showed you just exactly how to do it." He demonstrated in other ways that he loved me. He made things for me. He fixed broken things. He could fix anything. He would take me places with him and talk to me and teach me. He showed me how to do things. Those were the ways that I knew he loved me. In other ways, my mother showed that she loved me.

I want us to look at how we show that we love you. I want to share three specific ways your parents show their love. You may not have thought about these as expressions of love. Nevertheless, they are truly ways that your family shows that they care about you.

They Discipline You

One way your parents show they love you is by the discipline they give you. Real love carries with it discipline. The Greeks have different words for "love." One is for sexual attraction, ἔρος (*eros*), which really is not love at all. The word φιλέω (*phileō*) means a tender feeling toward someone. That is the kind of affection we have toward our friends, our roommates, our families. Then there is the supreme word for "love," ἀγάπη (*agapē*). The basic meaning of this word is to put the other person's good before your own, to ask what would be better for the other person before doing what you want to do. That is the love which God commands.

The *agapē* kind of love has severity with it, as well as tenderness. I suppose some of the strongest language Jesus ever used was directed to the church of Laodicea in Revelation 3. He said, in effect, "You make Me sick to My stomach." Verse 16 says, "So because you are lukewarm, and neither hot nor cold, I will spit you out of My mouth." That is rather strong. Right after that, He emphasized that, as much as He loves, He reproves and disciplines (3:19).

Many times, the greatest sign of love that parents show is telling you "no." Our deep love is demonstrated by the discipline we give you. Proverbs 13:24 says, "He who withholds his rod hates his son, but he who loves him disciplines him diligently."

As a little boy, I thought that it would be fun to discipline my children. When I became a father, I thought, "This will really be great," but I learned that it really is not a bit of fun. I have heard people say they love their children so much that they cannot bear to discipline them. Well, if they really understood what it means to love them, they would force themselves to be firm and teach those children right from wrong.

It takes a lot more love sometimes to show discipline to our children than to let them do whatever they want. When your parents said, "This will hurt me worse than it does you," did you believe it? When my parents said that, I always thought, "Well, why don't we just forget about the punishment then? Why should we all be miserable?" Since I have two children of my own, I know better. At times, after disciplining my children, I have felt sick in my stomach, with my hands trembling. The children seemed to forget all about it and go back to playing, but I have felt bad the rest of the night because of it.

Do you know why your mother and father sometimes make you stay at home when you want to go somewhere with friends? It is because they love you. Probably, they would rather let you leave the house because you are not any fun to be around at times like that. However, parents know that, while it may be an unpleasant evening for everyone, it is sometimes better for you not to go where you want to go. Do you know why your mother wants to know where you are going, who you are going with, what you plan to do when you get there, who else will be there, when you are coming home, and who will bring you home? Does she need all this information because she is writing a book? No, it is because she loves you and is concerned about your safety and well-being. If she did not love you, she would not care whether or not you came home. This is a sign of love.

In high school, I was in the band. One time, after a football game, I did not return home on the band bus, and I did not tell my parents that I would not be on the bus. I thought it would be all right if I rode home with a friend. He had a car, so we rode home with our girlfriends. We arrived at 12:30 instead of 10:30. After all, I was growing up. I was sixteen. It never occurred to me that anything was wrong with that until I got home. There was my mother, sitting on the front porch in the rocking chair. I thought, "Can't she sleep tonight? What is she doing out here at this time of night?"

Well, when I walked up that first step, I found out. She was showing me how much she loved me, but not in a way that I appreciated. She was concerned. Yes, that is one way that your parents show you they love you. They want you to be the best you possibly can be. They know that sometimes painful experiences are necessary to bring out the best in you.

THEY LET YOU GO

Sometimes parents may seem cruel. They take a little child off to school, leave him there, and go back home as if they didn't even have a child. It seems cruel for a bird to push a little fledgling out of the nest when it cannot yet fly. That mother bird knows that baby bird has to be on its own someday; it must learn to fly and find its own worms.

Even though we may not like it, as parents, we are trying to get you to the point that you no longer need us, to help you become independent. We try to give you enough responsibility that you can learn to live on your own. We do this because one day you will have to go on without us.

I guess the time I was the most disappointed with my father was when I was about six years old. A little boy across the street had my tricycle. He was a year or two older than I was and quite a bit bigger. My dad was home from work, so I thought we would get it back easily. I told my father the boy had my tricycle. He just told me to go get it myself. He said, "I'm not going over there to get your tricycle for you." I never was more disappointed in a man. He was bigger than that boy. I needed him, and he just sat there in a chair. On my own, I walked across the street, and there was that boy on my tricycle. I took a deep breath and firmly commanded, "Give me that tricycle!" I do not know what would have happened if he had refused, but he did not. He got off of that tricycle and ran home, and I triumphantly rode it back home. I couldn't understand it then, but my father did the right thing. He knew he would not always be available to do everything for me. He had to train me to be on my own. I did not know it until about fifteen years later; but, while I was out there trying to retrieve my tricycle, he was watching me through the front window.

If necessary, he was ready to intervene. I did not know he was there; at the time, I thought he was not even interested in my problems.

Perhaps the greatest act of love a father ever shows to a daughter is to stand before a preacher who is asking, "Who gives this woman in marriage?" and take his arm away from hers, and say, "Her mother and I." In this context, how beautiful are the words of Paul in 1 Corinthians 13:5: "[Love] does not seek its own"! One of the greatest acts of love your parents showed you may have been to help you pack a suitcase and send you away from home. Probably, many of them had tears streaming down their faces.

Your parents want what is best for you.

THEY FORGIVE YOU

Some people love the word "if": "I will love you *if* you will do this, *if* you will do that." That is not love. That is blackmail. Many of you may be experiencing another kind of love right now. That is love "because." Why do you love that person? "Because he or she is this or that." In contrast, there is love "in spite of." That is the only kind of love worth having. That is the kind of love wives and husbands must have for one another. That is the kind we mothers and fathers have for our children.

It is comforting to realize that—no matter where you go, no matter what trouble you get into—we still love you. Whatever you have done, whatever shame and reproach you may have brought upon the family, we love you. We love you in spite of it.

When I was in college, a boy came into my room after having a terrible day. I believe he had failed two tests, and his girlfriend had ended their relationship. He sat down on the edge of the bed, folded his hands on his knees, and said, "At least my mother loves me." That got him through the day.

If there ever was a scoundrel for a son, I think it was

Absalom. David had some wicked sons, but I believe the worst one was Absalom. He killed his brother Amnon. He tried to kill his father. He tried to take the kingdom away from him, and he actually did for a while. He even committed adultery with some of his stepmothers, the concubines of his father.

The final battle came in 2 Samuel 18: David's army against Absalom's army. When David's army went out to battle, what was the last thing David said to them? "Deal gently for my sake with the young man Absalom" (18:5). When they came back from the battle with the news that they had won, the first thing David asked was "Is it well with the young man Absalom?" (18:29).

When David heard that his son was dead, he went into his chamber and wept. He said, "O my son Absalom, my son, my son Absalom! Would I had died instead of you, O Absalom, my son, my son!" (18:33). As wicked and rebellious as that son was, he had a father who still loved him. He had a father who would have gladly died in his stead. Your parents love you.

THREE CHALLENGES

I want to say three things to you before I close. If your parents are Christians, you have an abundant privilege. Many of you are not taking advantage of the privileges that you have. Like the elder brother of the prodigal son, you are living beneath your privileges. Avail yourself of the counsel, wisdom, advice, love, and comfort that your parents can give you. I want to give you three challenges, and they all start with the letter "T."

Trust them. They are on your side. They always are, even though it may not look like it. They are seeking what is best for you. It is nice to have someone on your side.

I remember a girl who once needed help from her mother, as she was going through a time of depression. Her mother drove by herself all the way, six hundred miles, to be with her daughter. She stayed with her for a weekend, and then she went home. The very day she got home, her daughter called again and said, "Mother, I need you." She got in that car, and by herself, she drove back that day. That mother came into my office, and I talked with her. I had told the girl that I wanted to meet her. You have mothers and fathers like that too—parents who would do anything in the world to help you. You need to trust them.

Sometimes parents can give you reasons for the way they act, and sometimes they cannot. Sometimes the old saying "Because I said so" is all they can give you. When my daughter was eight years old, she came home one day and repeated a dirty joke she had heard somewhere. I looked at her and said, "Where did you hear that?" She said, "School." I told her not to tell that joke anymore. She asked why. "Because I said so" was my answer. She did not even realize it was a dirty joke. She did not even know why it was supposed to be funny. She just brought home something she had heard some of the older children telling.

At that particular age in her life, the only answer I could give her was "Because I said so." Later on, a parent might explain why that was inappropriate. Sometimes we can do that, but sometimes you have to trust us. I know you don't believe this, but we were once young too. We were teenagers a long time ago, and if you will listen to us, we will keep you from making some of the same mistakes we have made.

Tell them the truth. We parents cannot help you if you are not truthful with us. Parents get upset because they love you. I can be perfectly rational about anybody else's children, but I am emotionally involved with my own. Do you not think that is why God gets so angry with us? Is it not because of His love? If He did not love us so much, He would not get so angry with us. He loves you, and that is why He is so concerned. That is why His heart is hurt, and that is why He is angry sometimes. Tell the truth, no matter how much it hurts. Remember that, whatever the reaction is, it is because your parents really care.

Turn to them. Somebody said that young people need a place to stand. I agree with that. However, I am convinced that, more than that, young people need a place to turn. Many young people have come to me desperate because they thought they had nowhere to turn for help. Some have even contemplated suicide. They thought they had no one who cared about them.

I empathize with the desperate feeling that there is no place to turn and nowhere to look—but there is a place to turn. Do you have a mother and a father? The story of the prodigal son would be quite a different story if, when the boy was in the pig pen and said, "I ought to arise and go to my father," he had had no father. However, when he returned home and was yet far off, his father saw him and was moved with compassion. He ran and embraced the young man and kissed him (Luke 15:20). That boy turned to the right place. That father loved his son.[1]

When my son was about four, I was trying to get him to go to bed one night, which was always an ordeal. He had asked for his third drink of water and was brushing his teeth for the second time. As a last resort, he began a theological discussion. We were standing in the bathroom, and I was trying to turn the light off. He said, "Daddy, when I die, will I go to heaven to be with God and Jesus?" I stopped and took my hand off the light switch. I said, "Yes, God being your helper—God being *our* helper—you will be a Christian, and you will go to heaven to be with God and Jesus." He said, "Well, Daddy, when I do, I want you to go with me because I am scared of those big men."

That deeply touched my heart, although I did not say much to him then. That is what a home is all about. If we have missed heaven, our home has missed it all. God being our helper, we Christian mothers and fathers will die and go with

---

[1] Even if you have lost your parents, you probably have other family members who care about you. If you are a Christian, then you have many fellow Christians who can love you as a mother or a father would.

you children to heaven. You have a place to turn. No place in the world is better for you to turn than to the Father in heaven.

QUESTIONS

1. How did Abraham show his fear of God and love for his son (Genesis 22)?

2. How did Rizpah show her love for her sons (2 Samuel 21)?

3. How did the Shunammite woman show her love for her son (2 Kings 4)?

4. What was so surprising about the interaction between the Syrophoenician woman and Jesus (Matthew 15; Mark 7)?

5. Why is parental discipline a way of showing love?

6. How does the role of a parent fit into the idea of letting children go?

7. Of what three things should children avail themselves in relation to their parents?

3
Ten Commandments For Youth #1

"But seek first His kingdom and His righteousness, and all these things will be added to you" (Matthew 6:33).

When Moses went up on Mount Sinai, the Lord gave him ten commandments that served as the basis of the whole law of Moses. I have ten commandments for you young people that I hope will serve as the foundation and guideline for your lives for as long as you are on this earth. Make a point to remember them, and try as hard as you can every day to live by them.

PUT FIRST THINGS FIRST

Number one, put first things first. You can't possibly do everything you want to in this life. You girls cannot date every boy who calls you up. You just have to disappoint a few of them and then choose the one you want. You boys cannot go with all the girls who are wanting you to ask them out. You have to break the hearts of the others and choose just one. You cannot wear all the clothes you have at the same time or eat all the food you would like to eat or take all the classes you would like to take. You cannot go to all the Christian colleges you would like to attend. You have to choose what you are going to do.

You know, young people, I really believe that the key to

a successful and happy life is the ability to choose the things that really matter. In Philippians 1:9, 10, Paul was praying that the brethren there would learn to distinguish the things that differ. That literally means to be able to tell what is more important from what is less important. I heard a poem that illustrates what I am trying to say:

> Pussy cat, pussy cat, where have you been?
> I've been to London to look at the queen.
> Pussy cat, pussy cat, what did you there?
> I frightened a little mouse under her chair.

Of all the things the cat could have seen at the queen's palace, do you know what she saw? A mouse. She could have stayed at home and seen a mouse, couldn't she? Do you know why that cat saw a mouse? Because that is what cats like. They are interested in mice.

Some people come to Harding University and find the gymnasium and play ball all semester. We have these swings out on campus that are just big enough for two people. Some of them find those swings. A fellow finds a sweet little thing to sit with, and all semester they swing back and forth, back and forth. Some find the bed and stay in it most of the time. Some find the television in the lobby and sit in front of it. A few find the cafeteria and sit there and "pig out" every chance they get. Every once in a while, some strange person finds the library and actually makes some decent grades. What I am trying to get you to see is the importance of choosing that which is more important over that which is less important. Most of you are not having to deal with the problem of "Should I do a good thing or a bad thing?" but "Should I do a good thing or a better thing?"

A good illustration of that is in the Bible. In Luke 10, Mary was in the living room talking to Jesus about the Bible; Martha was in the kitchen fixing dinner. The biscuits needed to be taken out of the oven, the pie was burning, the sweet potatoes were sticking, and whatever else was happening. All of a sudden in exasperation, Martha ran in and said, "Lord, do You not care that my sister has left me to do all the serving alone? Then tell her to help me" (10:40). I think it is funny that Martha didn't say, "Mary, get in here and help me." She said, "Lord, make her come in here!" I guess she thought she would come nearer listening to Him. Anyway, Jesus said, "Martha, Martha, . . ." Did you ever notice when Jesus tenderly rebuked someone, He repeated the name? "Martha, Martha, you are worried and bothered about so many things; but only one thing is necessary, for Mary has chosen the good part, which shall not be taken away from her" (10:41, 42). It is a matter of choosing what is better. As nice as it was to fix a good meal for the Lord, something was more important than that: listening to what the Lord had to say.

Coming back to Moses' Ten Commandments, the children of Israel were there at the foot of Mount Sinai. That mountain was quaking and trembling, the voice of the trumpet was heard, and the lightning flashes and smoke were seen. What was the first thing they heard out of that mountain? Do you know? "I am the LORD your God, who brought you out of the land of Egypt, out of the house of slavery. You shall have no other gods before Me" (Exodus 20:2, 3). Do you know what God was saying in that first commandment? Put first things first. You have heard people say God is everywhere. I will tell you a place that God refuses to be. He refuses to be in second place. He must be first in your life. It is a matter of priority; that is all it is.

Our Lord said the same thing in Matthew 6:33. He said it is all right to make provision for what you will eat and drink and what you will wear, but that is not the most important thing. He said, "But seek first His kingdom and His righteousness, and all these things will be added to you." Put first things first. I was told that a manufacturer of Heinz pickles had a jar of pickles on his desk, and when anyone would come into the president's office, he would see that jar of pickles. He had written on that jar, "God first, others second, pickles third." There is not a thing wrong with pickles as long as they stay third, but it is really a problem when they get up in first or second place. Young people, one of the most important commandments of the ten is the first one: Put first things first in your life.

Do Not Forsake the Assembling of the Saints

Number two, do not forsake the assembling of the saints. You never thought that would be one of the ten, did you? Let me tell you why it is so important for young people. You are at an extremely crucial age. Most of you have gone to church since you can't remember. You have been very faithful in your attendance. Do you know why? Because you were too little to leave home. Mama and Daddy just picked you up and put you in the car, isn't that right? They dragged you out and set you on the seat and said, "Be still."

When our children were little, we would get them up and say, "Eat your bread"; "Chew your toast"; "Brush your teeth"; "Put on your shoes"; "Comb your hair"; "Get in the car." They would say, "Where are we going?" Our answer was "We're going to church." They went to church regularly. When you are young, you go to church because Mama and Daddy take you. It is their faith—but young people, you are reaching the stage in life when if you attend church, it will be your own idea. It will be your own choice. That is why it is so critical at this stage in your life. You have to confront the question "What am I going to do?" No longer will you have Mama and Daddy saying, "Get up and get ready for church." No longer are they going to be getting you up in the mornings in a few years. You will have to get yourself up. What are you going to do then? Let me give you some reasons you should be faithful to the Lord's assembly.

The Bible commands it. Hebrews 10:25 says, ". . . not forsaking our own assembling together. . . ." That does not say "Sunday morning." It means the act of coming together. When the saints come together, we need to be there.

You need that encouragement. A preacher visited a man because he had quit going to church. He told the preacher, "I can be just as good a Christian here at home as I can at church. I don't have to go and worship with all the others." They were sitting in front of a fireplace, and the preacher reached in with a poker. He pulled out the hottest coal of fire and set it apart all by itself. Before long, it didn't even glow anymore. Before long, it was stone cold. The fellow said, "I get the point. I'll be there Sunday." You need the encouragement of fellow Christians.

You need to set an example for others. I heard about a man in the church who could neither hear nor see, but he always went to church and sat on the front row. Someone asked him why. He didn't even know what was going on. He said, "I want the people to see whose side I am on. That is why I'm here."

Young people, I am not so concerned about the fact that you don't go to church as I am why you don't go to church. I don't really think that you are going to heaven because you punched the clock and you logged 97,000 hours of sitting in church. I don't think that is going to do it. What bothers me is what keeps you from the Lord's assembly. What bothers me is the fact that there are things more important in your life than coming and worshiping with the saints.

Girls, let me talk to you a minute. What would you think if that boyfriend took you home tonight and, as he let you in the door, he said to you, "Have I got to come back again this week?" What would you say to him? You would probably say, "No, and for that matter, next week either." Isn't that right? How do you think the Lord must feel whenever some people say, "Have I got to come back again tonight?" I wonder if the Lord in heaven might look down and say, "No, forget it. If that is all you care about, forget it." We sing, "Oh, how I love Jesus"; "How sweet would by thy children's fate if we, like them, could die for Thee." And then we say, "Have I got to come back on Wednesday night?" What keeps that boy coming back to your door, girls? He is there morning, noon, and night, isn't he? Do you give gold stars or blue ribbons for perfect attendance? Is that what gets him there? No, it is commitment. He is there on that doorstep, but Mama runs him off. He is back on there as soon as she gets back in the house. As soon as he gets home, he is on the phone. He hasn't heard your voice in five minutes. Now, that is a commitment. That is love. When we have people who love the Lord, they are not going to be fussing and complaining about having to go to church. They have no other place they would rather be and no other people they would rather be with. There is nothing in the world they would enjoy more than the fellowship of one another.

I am not going to tell you that every service of the Lord's church is a good time. Honestly, it is not. When my son was about eighteen, we were walking home by the tennis courts; and in a rather confidential way, he said, "Daddy, I hate to tell you this. I get so bored sometimes at church." I said, "Really? Well, Alan, I get bored sometimes too." He looked at me and said, "You, a preacher and a Bible teacher, get bored at church?" I said, "Yes, Alan, there are times when I get bored out of my gourd. There are times when I sit there and wonder when it will ever be over." I am not going to say that if you are really holy you will be highly entertained every time the doors are open. We go even when we don't feel like it because we know that is where we should be. We sit there respectfully and endure some things that we would just as soon not endure because we love the Lord and we love our brethren. Young people, we attend sometimes because we want to, because we discipline ourselves, because we know that is what the Lord wants us to do. We know that we need to be there to encourage our brothers and sisters in Christ.

A little fellow named "Benny" lived across the street from me when I was a child. One Wednesday night, I had to quit playing and go in to get ready for church. Benny was still out playing. I said, "Don't you all go to church on Wednesday night? Don't you have to get ready?" He said, "We never go on Wednesday night. I can just play until bedtime." I said, "You mean where you go to church you all don't even have meetings on Wednesday night?" He said, "Yes, we have them; but we never go. It is just for those who are old and about to die and really want to go to heaven, and we never go." His mother and daddy weren't fooling him, were they? He could see right through their pretense of religion. Yes, that is really true. Only those who really want to go show up. I hope that you are some of those who really want to go.

THOU SHALT LOOK LIKE A CHRISTIAN

Number three, thou shalt look like a Christian. I am talking about your appearance. I preached this sermon at the College church, and right after that I gave some teenagers a ride to a skating party. I shouldn't have done this, but I was testing them to see how I came across. One girl couldn't remember a thing I said all through the sermon except one point. She said, "I remember one thing you said, 'Don't wear the devil's uniform.'" I am a member of the army of the Lord, and I don't want to run around waving the devil's flag and wearing the devil's uniform and telling everybody, "I may look like one of the devil's men, but I am a good Christian. You can't tell by my appearance, but I am a good Christian."

Years ago, boys' hair was a bigger deal than it is now. I remember I was in a gospel meeting north of here, and we had a youth meeting in the afternoon. All they wanted to talk about was hair. They had a problem with boys wearing long hair. The elders told the boys, "You are not going to wait on the table until you cut your hair." The boys said, "We are not going to cut our hair." We argued about that about forty-five minutes; and I stood up and said, "Boys, I will tell you exactly when your hair is too long. Your hair is too long when it is a stumbling block between you and your influence for Christ."

Frankly, I don't think that verse in 1 Corinthians 11 is saying that a boy has to wear a flattop. If some of you wore more hair, you might look better. It might cover up more of your face! If you want to look like a shaggy dog, that is your problem. When your appearance detracts from your influence for Christ, it is a sin. It is a sin—not because you have long hair. It is a sin because your appearance is more important to you than your influence for the Lord.

A student who came into my office really looked as if he was in trouble. He said, "I have to talk to you." I thought, "What in the world has this fellow done?" I could just imagine all kinds of things: drinking, dope, immorality, sex. He said, "I preach out from Searcy." I said, "Yes, I know." He said, "We are having a campaign for Christ. We are going to knock on every door in that community." I said, "That is wonderful." He said, "They want me to cut my beard off before I knock doors out there. What should I do?" And I almost laughed in his face with a sigh of relief. "You mean that is what you are so worried about?" I said, "Cut it off." He said, "But I spent all summer growing it." I said, "You can grow another one next summer. It will grow back. Cut it off if that stands between you and your influence for the Lord in that community." It is not just the way you look; it is not the matter that you have two inches of hair on your head or on your chin. The issue is this: What is this doing for your influence for the Lord?

Now, girls, let me say some things to you. First Timothy 2:9 says that girls should adorn themselves in modest apparel. That word "modest" means "appropriate." Wear what is appropriate. That is what it is talking about. This may be a surprise to some of you. Paul was telling women not to wear too many clothes. Nearly every time we quote that verse today, it is concerning women wearing too few clothes. You can be immodest by overdressing or by underdressing, either way. Girls, I would be embarrassed if I were a girl and someone had to speak to me about the way I dressed because I was dressing in a suggestive and lewd manner. I would want to be wearing a uniform that shows I am a Christian girl, that I am wholesome and pure. You are advertising what you are by the way you look. What kind of a uniform are you running around in?

A girl was angered because a man downtown made an indecent proposal to her. She ran home and told her mama, who said, "We'll just tell Daddy about this." When her daddy came home, she told him. Her daddy said, "He shouldn't have done that, but look at the way you are dressed. Look at the girls you were with. Think about the flirtatious way you girls were behaving." He said, "You probably never knew it, but you were advertising. You were sending out signals to that fellow: 'I am the sort of girl who would invite that kind of a proposition.'" Girls, you may never mean to do it; but by the way you dress, or don't dress, you may be sending this message. Guys may be picking up on those signals. I wouldn't be caught in the devil's uniform. I would want to wear the Lord's uniform. I would never be caught waving the devil's flag. If I had to keep apologizing to people for the way I look, I would change the way I look.

THOU SHALT TALK LIKE A CHRISTIAN

Number four, thou shalt talk like a Christian. Remember when Peter was warming himself by the coals the night Jesus was being tried? One of the maids came by and said, "You are one of them." He said, "No, I am not." Another one came by and said, "I saw you in the garden with Him." He said, "I was not there. I don't know the man." Then a third one came by, and she said, "Surely you too are one of them; for even the way you talk gives you away" (Matthew 26:73). Then he began to curse and swear, "I do not know the man!" (26:74). If you are afraid that your speech is going to betray you as being a servant of the Lord, just curse and swear. I don't think anybody would ever accuse you of being a child of His.

Really, though, that was not what the maid meant when

she said this to Peter. She meant, "Your accent gives you away." Peter was from Galilee, up north; and Jesus was crucified in Judea, Jerusalem, down south. Would you believe that those Jews up north had a different accent from the Jews down south? Have you ever noticed how funny these people up north talk? Have you noticed how odd those southerners sound? I remember I was preaching at one place, and a lady said, "I can hardly understand you; you have such an accent." I didn't have the accent. She was the one who had the accent. I don't have an accent. I talk the way you are supposed to talk. Isn't that the way you think about yourself? I was preaching in Illinois about two years before I went to Harding; and one of the ladies said, "About the time we taught you how to talk, you are going to go back south and forget it all." That is what the accusation was against Peter. "You have that Yankee brogue. We have the southern drawl here in Judea." ". . . the way you talk gives you away" (Matthew 26:73).

Young people, your speech gives you away. The way you talk and the way you dress betray you as a child of God or a child of the devil. I see no excuse whatever for filthy, vulgar talk. If I were going to go to hell, I would pick a better reason than that to go. Cursing and swearing is about the dumbest sin that I can think of. It doesn't make anyone think any more of you. It doesn't show you are very smart. It is generally a sign of a limited vocabulary. You can teach a parrot to curse. There are only about thirty good curse words, and I already know all of them. You do too. All you do is just rearrange them. That is no big deal. I don't understand why anyone wants to do that. That is such a dumb thing. If I were going to sin for a living, I would put that on the bottom of the list. It makes some people dislike you. It doesn't make anybody who is anybody think any more of you; it doesn't show you are smart; it doesn't show you have good breeding; it doesn't show you have good sense. It just shows you are filthy.

Your words are a mirror to your soul. People can't see what is inside of you. Aren't you glad they can't? When you open your mouth, they can hear what is inside of you. If I had all that filth inside of me, I wouldn't want anybody to know it. I wouldn't open my mouth and reveal it. I would try to keep my mouth shut.

Dare to Be Different

Number five, dare to be different. The devil wants you to be like him and all of his henchmen. The world wants to force you into its mold. Young people, at your age in life, one of the strongest influences to shape your living and thinking is peer pressure. If you don't go along with the others, you are a "chicken," you are a "turkey," you are a "squirrel." The devil doesn't like those who are different. The devil wants you to conform to the world around you. I honestly believe, young people, one of the greatest pressures you have is the pressure to conform.

In 1 Samuel 8, Samuel was old and his sons were not the kind of men to judge the people. So the people came and said, "Give us a king." Samuel said, "No, you shouldn't have a king." They answered, "Yes, give us a king that we also may be like all the nations." They were saying, "We want to be like everybody else." That is a good reason for having a king, isn't it?

How many young people have said to their parents, "Why can't I? Everybody else does." Have any of you ever said that? We all have. If everybody else does it, we want to do it. Romans 12:2 says, "And do not be conformed to this world, but be transformed by the renewing of your mind, so that you may prove what the will of God is, that which is good and acceptable and perfect." I like the way Phillips translates that: "Don't let the world around you squeeze you into its own mould." In other words, dare to stand and be different. God's people are different.

Everybody was supposed to bow down to the golden image that Nebuchadnezzar set up in Daniel 3. Anyone who didn't bow down to the image would be thrown into a fiery furnace. That didn't bother Shadrach, Meshach, and Abednego. At the sound of the trumpets and the other musical instruments, everybody else bowed down—but not Shadrach, Meshach, and Abednego. I might not have bowed down to the image, but I don't think I would have been standing up so conspicuously. That would have been a good time to tie my shoe or to hunt four-leaf clovers or to look for my contact lens. If nothing else, I could bow down and pray to God to help me get through this, couldn't I? I would find some way not to stick out like a sore thumb, wouldn't you? They didn't. They dared to be different.

In Daniel 6, an edict was given that, for thirty days, anyone who prayed to any god or man besides King Darius would be thrown into a den of lions. Daniel went to his home and, as he always did, prayed toward Jerusalem three times a day with his window open. I believe I would have prayed to God, but that would have been a good time to close the window—with the dust coming in and the draft. Better still, I would have waited until I could blow out the lamp and give my silent prayer in the bed when nobody else could see me. I could have sneaked in a prayer—but Daniel dared to be different.

It takes a lot of courage to be different, young people. I really understand you on that. I remember back when I was a teenager, one time at a band party, some of the others were dancing, and I was interested in a certain girl. I remember the boys dancing with her, and I was sitting over there with tears welling up in my eyes because I couldn't dance and there was that boy going off with that girl I wanted. Now don't feel sorry for me. I got married anyway and lived happily ever after. I got a girl twice as good as that one. The Lord pretty well takes care of these things. If you give up something for the Lord, He will give you something twice as good. Still, I can remember that pressure. I can remember sitting there thinking, "It's not fair. It's not fair." I can remember a lot of experiences like that. You can too, can't you?

Young people, you are going to have to be strong enough

to say "no." The world has put "chicken" on the wrong bird. You are not a chicken if you say "no." You are a chicken if you don't have enough backbone to say "no." The chicken is the little fellow who runs along with everybody else and doesn't have the courage to say "no." I think a man who stands up and says, "I will not do it," knowing he will be cut off from the others, knowing he will be made fun of, knowing he will be excluded and maybe even lose a girlfriend or his friends, is the man to be admired. That is the young man or the young woman I respect. That is the kind of person the Lord loves.

The Bible says we are a peculiar people. That doesn't mean we ought to see how odd we can be. Most of us are odd enough without trying. It means, literally, that we belong to God. This is my peculiar watch—not because it is strange, but because it belongs to me. In the Bible, "peculiar," as in Titus 2:14 in the King James Version, means belonging particularly to God. We are different. We have a different Master. We live by a different set of rules. We live by the word of God. We belong to a different kingdom. We have a different home. We have different goals and aims in life. Of course we are different. If the people around us don't see we are different, something is wrong. We must stand up and be different. Dare to be different. Being different is no compliment in the world. If that girl comes in from dating you and her friends say, "How was he?" and she says, "He was different," you didn't do very well. You struck out because that is no compliment. God's people are different. They march to the sound of a different drummer. They are headed to a different destination. They live by different rules and commandments. I want to encourage you to have that strength of mind and courage you need to stand up and be different.

When the children of Israel worshiped the golden calf, Moses was so infuriated that he broke the stone tablets. Then, when he challenged them in Exodus 32 saying, "Who is on the Lord's side?" the Levites stood beside him. I give to you that same challenge. Who is on the Lord's side? Who has the cour-

BUILDING A GODLY HOME

age to take a stand for the Lord? Who is on the Lord's side? Maybe you can take that stand for Him today.

QUESTIONS

1. What is the key to a happy and successful life?

2. What does the story of Mary and Martha in Luke 10 teach us about choosing?

3. Where must God be in our lives?

4. What are three reasons we should be faithful to the Lord's assembly?

5. As with the way we dress, how does our speech betray us?

6. The Bible says we are to be what kind of people (Titus 2:14)?

4
Ten Commandments For Youth #2

But the LORD said to Samuel, "Do not look at his appearance or at the height of his stature, because I have rejected him; for God sees not as man sees, for man looks at the outward appearance, but the LORD looks at the heart" (1 Samuel 16:7).

We have already covered five commandments to young people. Now we want to look at five more.

BEAUTIFY THE INNER PERSON

The sixth commandment is to beautify the inner person. So much emphasis is placed on the outward appearance! You must be beautiful or handsome, or you will never amount to anything—so you are told. Don't call me "ugly." Call me "clumsy." Call me "short." Don't call me "ugly." That word is the greatest scourge upon mankind today, isn't it? This puts a lot of pressure on young people. When you get older and set in your ways, you don't have to be all that pretty. You are already married. You have your girlfriend or boyfriend caught, and you are already settled. At your age, though, the outward appearance seems to be of the utmost importance. We boys have the same feeling that if we don't grow to be six foot five and weigh 280 pounds, we are going to be a "peewee," and no one will like us. We are going to be ugly!

In 1 Samuel 16, the prophet Samuel went down to Bethlehem to anoint a king who would take the place of Saul. Jesse was invited, and one of his sons would be the next king. He had eight sons. The first one came by: a big, tall, good-looking fellow named "Eliab." Samuel thought as he looked at his outward appearance, "Surely the Lord's anointed is before me." Then, in 1 Samuel 16:7, God said, "Do not look at his appearance or at the height of his stature, because I have rejected him; for God sees not as man sees, for man looks at the outward appearance, but the LORD looks at the heart."

I have wondered, if just for one day in our lives, what a difference it would make if God would let us look on the outside the way we really are on the inside. Some of those beautiful, handsome, most fascinating people would be the most hideous that you have ever seen. Some of those plain, ordinary people you never paid any attention to would be the most beautiful people you ever laid eyes on. I honestly believe that. If you and I would spend just half the time trying to make the inside of us as pretty as we do the outside, we would all be ten times better off. In 1 Peter 3, Peter was talking to the women about this. In verses 3 and 4 he said,

> Your adornment must not be merely external—braiding the hair, and wearing gold jewelry, or putting on dresses; but let it be the hidden person of the heart, with the imperishable quality of a gentle and quiet spirit, which is precious in the sight of God.

Young people, when I set out as a teenager looking for a girl, I had just two qualifications: One was that she had to be a girl, and the second was that she had to be pretty. That is all I ever thought about, except a third one was that she had to be willing to go out with me. That sort of cut the field down. I never thought about other things. I would have ended up with the same girl I have now, and she is certainly a beautiful lady; but, let me tell you, there are things about her that I appreciate more than her beauty. I appreciate the fact that she is a Christian. I appreciate her love for me and her love for our children. I appreciate the way she loves the Lord. I appreciate the fact that she is considerate and kind. I appreciate how sympathetic she is when I need someone to be sympathetic. Those are the things that really matter in life.

I would like to encourage you not to get so hung up upon the externals. These externals are not going to last, young people. That black, curly hair that is so fascinating, that you girls love to run your fingers through, one day is going to turn gray—or worse than that, turn loose. Those big, manly shoulders and powerful muscles one day are going to get soft. He is not going to lose them; they are just going to drop and hang right around the belt. That manly chin that shows firmness of character is going to have some companions; a double and a triple and others will join it. I will not go into all of the details, but some of you girls aren't going to fare much better. You are not always going to be the beautiful things you are now. Young people, there is a beauty that every one of you can have—a beauty that outlasts all of the others and grows more beautiful the longer you live. That is the beauty of spirit, the beauty of heart.

Perhaps you have been around some people whom you saw for the first time and were smitten by how beautiful or handsome they were; but the more you were around them, the uglier they got. You ended up wondering, "What did I ever see in him [or her]?" Maybe you have been around other people whom you never paid much attention to at first and never thought they were all that attractive, but the more you were around them, the better looking they got. My mother-in-law used to call that "bearing acquaintance." Do you know what it is? It is the beauty of the soul within them. That is what you need to look for in a person.

I am not downgrading beauty. I don't want to leave that impression at all. If you are good-looking, more power to you. I think we should all try to look as good as we can. However,

I do want to show you that there is a beauty a thousand times more important than that. Young people, if you are not going to be successful in life, it won't be because of what is on the outside. It will be because of what is on the inside. Commandment number six, spend time making the inside beautiful.

Honor Your Family

Commandment number seven, honor your family. You may expect me to say, as Exodus 20 does, "Honor your father and your mother" (verse 12), but I want to broaden that a little bit. You should be kind and considerate to your brothers and sisters, even if they are younger than you, even if they bug you. You may not realize at your age how much your younger brothers and sisters look up to you. Some of them think you are the greatest thing in the world. They will follow your example more quickly than they will follow Mother's and Daddy's. They would give anything in the world for a kind word from you, for approval from you, for even a sign that you care about them, for even a sign that you notice them. Let me encourage you to do that. Then, of course, there are your father and your mother. I have three points I want to make about that. *One is that you need to obey your mother and father.* Ephesians 6:1 says, "Children, obey your parents in the Lord, for this is right." It is important for young people to be submissive to their parents.

Many times, young people come to me complaining, "My mother and daddy won't let me do anything. They won't let me go places. They won't give me the freedom I think that I should have at my age. They won't let me have the car as I think they should." Do you want me to tell you young people how to get more privileges? Be faithful to the responsibilities you have. As the father of teenagers, I am more than glad to give our children liberty, but I give them liberty only when they have convinced me by their behavior that they are ready for it. In other words, if you don't know how to act with the car, we will have to keep it from you until you learn how to act. Then, maybe, we will try again when you get a little older. If you don't know how to act on a date, we will keep you home for a little while. You will grow up a little more, and then we will try it again. If you don't know how to act in church, you can come and sit with us until you learn how to act away from us. Then we will let you go back and sit away from us. Young people, that is the way we parents operate. Did you know that? When we can trust you to obey us and be responsible with the liberties we have given you, we will be glad to give you more. You don't think we sit with you just because we want to sit with you, do you? You don't think we are keeping you home just because we like to look at you, do you? No, we are doing that because you haven't convinced us that you are mature enough to go and do otherwise.

Your mothers and fathers will make mistakes with you. You got whippings you didn't deserve, and you should have gotten a few that you didn't get. They even out. Your parents will even make wrong decisions; they will tell you wrong things to do sometimes. Young people, the aggravating thing is they are right most of the time. About 80 to 90 percent of the time, they are right. We can thank them for not saying, "I told you so," every time, can't we? Do you know why they are right so much? It is not luck. They used to be teenagers too. It is hard for you to believe that they were anything but old men and women, but they were. They have been through all of that. They know exactly what you are going through, more than you will ever realize. They went through the same things and did a lot of dumb things. If you will listen to them, they can keep you from making the same dumb mistakes they did. Obey them.

The second point about your parents is this: *Level with them.* The one thing I would punish our children for more than anything else, I guess, would be lying to us. I would deal more severely with that than with any other misbehavior. Young people, we parents can help you only to the extent that we know the truth of the situation. If you will tell us the truth, we can help you; but if you are lying to us, we cannot help you. If you are devious, if you don't let us know where you are coming from and what you are doing, then that cuts us off. It is like going to the doctor. What do you think of someone going to the doctor and lying about everything? He says, "How do you feel?" And you say, "I feel great," when you are about to die. He pushes here and says, "Does that hurt?" "No, it doesn't hurt a bit," you say, though it is about to kill you. He sticks a thermometer in your mouth, and when he is not looking you stick it in ice water. Whom are you hurting? You really played a trick on the doctor, didn't you? Who is going to get sick and die—the doctor? When I go to the doctor, I tell him everything that I think is possibly wrong with me. I realize his ability to help me is in direct proportion to the knowledge he has. Young people, you need to let us parents trust you. However it may be, if you have Christian parents, or even parents who love you but are not Christians, it is far better for you to tell them the truth. They may raise the roof at first, but it is far better for you to tell them the truth than to lie to them.

A former student of mine named "Wayne" told a story that has meant a lot to me, and I want to share it with you. When he was young, he was accused of stealing some money at school; and the principal called his parents in. The parents sat down by little Wayne and said, "Wayne, whatever you do, don't lie to us. Tell us the truth, whatever it costs. Did you take the money?" He said, "Yes, I did." They worked it out so that they would pay back the stolen money, and then he would pay them back as he could earn it. He made it right. He said it was a while after that that he was accused of hurting a little girl on the playground. He was brought in to the principal again. The parents were brought in again. Once again the parents sat down with Wayne and said, "Wayne, did you hurt that little girl? Please don't lie to us. Whatever you do, don't lie to us." He said, "I never touched that girl." The parents said, "I believe you"; and Wayne said, "They believed me then because I had been truthful with them before."

Young people, if you have the trust of your parents, you have something that is really precious. Don't destroy it for anything in the world. How wonderful it is when you have such a relationship with your mother and daddy that they can believe and trust you! Don't ever do anything to destroy that. Obey them, level with them, and *third, love them*. You say, "Of course I love them." Let me suggest that you tell them that. They may faint, but go ahead and tell them that. When you get in tonight about one or two o'clock, wake them up and hug their necks. If you are not going home tonight, call them and tell them how much you love them. No, I am teasing.

Let me tell you something without getting overly sentimental. Don't wait until it is too late to tell them that you love them. I am firmly convinced that many tears at funerals are not tears of grief but tears of guilt. I have seen people, weeping beside a dead mother or father, who would give anything in the world if they could bring their parents back for just five or ten minutes to tell them how much they loved them. I have made myself a pledge that if and when I stand beside the lifeless form of my mother or father (and thanks be to God they are both living and in good health now), there is one regret I will not have. I will never regret that I didn't tell them I loved them because I have made doubly sure they know that. My wife's father died in August of 1979. We sat beside the bed of my dying father-in-law, and I told him I loved him so much for being the father he was to me and to my wife. Then the thought hit me: "If this is the first time I have ever really expressed my love for him, this is a rather empty sound, isn't it? If I haven't convinced him in the last nineteen years by the way I have treated him as his son-in-law, then I should just as well shut up as I sit by his deathbed."

Brother J. D. Bales was reared by a grandmother. His parents were killed in a train wreck when he was about eleven. He decided in his older days he would write his grandmother. He never had thanked her for all that she had done for him, and so he wrote her a letter. He didn't know it at that time, but she was on her deathbed. She kept that letter on her nightstand and showed it to all the people who came by. He said if he had just waited another month or two, that debt of gratitude would never have been paid. How thankful he was that he had written that letter!

A student of mine at Harding, named "Larry," worked one summer in a funeral home. One of his jobs was to close the caskets each evening after people had left. As he came upon one, he noticed a piece of paper lying on the corpse. He picked up the piece of paper and read, "Dear Father, I am so sorry for all the trouble I caused you. I love you." The daughter had signed her name. She had waited a little bit late to write that letter. I hope you will make a pledge within your heart that when your parents depart this life—and may it be many, many years from now—you will never have the regret that you didn't tell them how much you loved them.

BE A SOUL-WINNER

Number eight, be a soul-winner. Who do you think are the most receptive prospects for conversion—the over-seventy age group or the forty-to-sixty age group? No. The younger people are the most receptive. Who do you think are our best missionaries to that group—the old salts? No. The young people are. Young people, you can reach souls that your preacher can't reach. You can talk to those people where they are. You can invite them to come to worship, and they will come with you. If we invited them, they wouldn't come. Have you ever thought of the fact that you are a soul-winner or should be now? We generally say, "After I graduate from high school, go to a Christian college and major or minor in Bible, and I'm at a church another five or ten years, then I will go out and try to win souls." Oh, no, do it now.

TEN COMMANDMENTS FOR YOUTH #2

A girl I know in California went to her mother complaining, "There aren't any Christians in my class." Her mother said, "Why complain about it? Go make some." She converted two that year. There were three at the end of the year. She had gone out and converted them herself. Are you complaining because there aren't any Christians where you live? Well, make some. Have you ever tried? Have you ever really communicated a love and concern for someone? Have you ever taken the time to invite them or ask them if they would talk with you about the Bible? You might be surprised at how receptive some of your friends are. Some will laugh at you, but that won't hurt you. You will get over it.

One of the best things you can do is to live the right life in front of them, to be an example. A girl named "Brenda," who was from Michigan, came to Harding several years ago. She wasn't a Christian. In fact, she was an agnostic. She came to Harding as a sophomore, transferring out of a state university. She was in my Bible class, and I tried to convince her there is a God. We would talk about evidences of Christianity. I used the cosmological and teleological arguments; and if I could have understood it, I would even have tried the ontological argument on her. Her good fortune was to be in a suite in the dormitory with three beautiful Christian girls and to have the most Christian roommate you could pick. She was in one of the very best social clubs for young girls on the campus. She saw something in their lives that she didn't have, and she wanted it in her life. I don't have to tell you that in January of that school year, she was baptized one Wednesday night. It wasn't because of all my great wisdom that I laid on her. It was because there were people who lived Christ in front of her. They were the real soul-winners. Though I did the baptizing. I don't think I will get much credit for that one.

At the end of that year, I did something I don't normally do on a final exam. I wrote down on the test, "This will in no way affect your grade. Tell what you would rather have emphasized in this class more than was." I was trying to tailor the course to their needs and interests. I left about a third of a page blank. I was grading papers late that night. After grading about fifty or sixty of them, I get bleary-eyed and dull. I came to Brenda's paper; and she had written across that whole third of a page in great big letters, "You are the light of the world." When I read that, I felt a shiver run all over me. "You are the light of the world" (Matthew 5:14a).

Young people, I don't believe I could overimpress that on you. You are the light of the world. In the communities where you live, in the churches you attend, the schools that you go to, you are the light of the world. Jesus says, "A city set on a hill cannot be hidden. . . . Let your light shine before men in such a way that they may see your good works, and glorify your Father in heaven" (Matthew 5:14b–16). Many never read the Gospel According to Matthew, Mark, Luke, or John; but they do read the gospel according to you. Be a soul-winner, commandment number eight.

WATCH THE COMPANY YOU KEEP

Number nine, watch the company you keep. First Corinthians 15:33 says, "Do not be deceived: 'Bad company corrupts good morals.'" You cannot keep from being influenced by the people you are around. That is one thing we parents are so concerned about. Have you ever noticed that? Whenever you want to go somewhere, Mama or Daddy says, "Who are you going with?" Isn't that the first thing they say? "Well, who is that? Whose kid is that?" My daddy said that his daddy used to say, "Whose kid is that?" to him; and he thought, "Well, who cares whose kid it is? I don't know his ancestors." Then I started going around; and my daddy would say to me when I would pick out friends, "Whose kids are those?" Now would you believe our children talk about some of their friends, and what is the first thing I say? "Whose kids are those?" Why? Just because we are nosy? No, because we realize the importance of the people you are with and how they influence your thinking and behavior. Nearly every time young people get in trouble, the first thing you will hear is this: "I got in the wrong crowd." They forget they are a part of that crowd, don't they?

I don't mean to imply that you should be snooty and not associate with anybody. You should reach out to everyone and be a friend, even to the worst of sinners—but, young people, choose your close friends very carefully. Our Lord was a friend to publicans and sinners, and He was criticized for it by the Pharisees and the scribes. However, Mark 3:14 says that Jesus chose twelve to be with Him. He chose His close companions carefully. Choose your close friends carefully.

A little girl died in a neighborhood, and the parents of the little girl let the playmates compose the epitaph for her tombstone. Do you know what they decided to put on it? "It was easier to be good when she was around." Have you ever noticed, young people, when you get with certain people, you nearly always get in trouble; and when you get with other people, you don't get in trouble? That ought to tell you something. A bell ought to go off in your head. I remember when our girl was about ten. There were these little girls, and every time she would go out with them to play, she would get in trouble. I called her in and said, "Lori, have you ever noticed when you are out with so-and-so, that you get in trouble, and when you are off playing with so-and-so, that you don't get in trouble and we get along? That ought to teach you something."

What kind of people are you with? You need to be with the people who uphold the things that are positive, that are spiritually uplifting, not people who are trying to tear down your principles and your morals and trying to get you to go places you know you shouldn't go and do things you know you shouldn't do. That kind of friend you can do without. "He who walks with wise men will be wise, but the companion of fools will suffer harm" (Proverbs 13:20). Choose your company wisely.

Keep Yourself Pure

Number ten, keep yourself pure. Young people, sex is not dirty, nasty, or shameful. Sex is something beautiful. God made it. When God made Eve and brought her to Adam, He made sex right there. He could have brought another man to Adam. Aren't you glad that He didn't, fellows? He said, "Adam, I want you to meet Eve. She is like you, but she is a little different"; and Adam said, "Hot dog!" That is not in there, but I am sure that is exactly what he said.

Sex is beautiful. Boys should like girls. You aren't a dirty old man if you like girls. Girls should like boys. You're not wicked if you like boys. The one to worry about is the boy who doesn't like girls and a girl who doesn't like boys. That is the one I am worried about. This attraction is normal. It is something that is beautiful and wonderful. Nothing is wrong with it unless we abuse the laws that God has laid down. Sex is an appetite, and there is a right time and a wrong time to satisfy that appetite. Hunger is an appetite. There is a right time and a wrong time to satisfy it. Right now is not the time to satisfy your hunger. About 4:30 to 6:00 is the time to do that. We don't want anyone satisfying his appetite during a Bible class or a worship service. That would be out of place. In its right place, it is all right.

Sex is like that. Young people, you really are in an awkward stage because you are at the age when you are physically ready to get married. Your body is just as ready for sexual fulfillment as it ever will be. You are ready for marriage physically, but you are not ready mentally. You never will be ready financially. You are not ready emotionally. You are not ready chronologically. You have a period of tension there, maybe five or eight years, when you are ready physically but not otherwise. This, more than likely, will be one of your biggest temptations during this period of your life. God hasn't given you something to fight with all the rest of your life. He has given you a perfectly acceptable outlet for all of this drive and desire and passion. It is in the love between a man and a woman in the framework of marriage. All the shame and the stigma come from using it outside of the framework of marriage. Premarital sex, homosexuality, bestiality, adultery—these are the sins. What are they? They are abuses of where God has put sex.

Young people, let me plead with you to keep yourself pure. What could you give that man or woman whom you will marry someday? What would be the greatest gift you could bestow upon him or her? I think it would be your virginity. I promise you, young people, I promise you that if you do lose that, you will regret it. I am 101 percent sure that you will. I have had too many people talk to me. Girls come in weeping over the mistakes they have made, wanting to know if they can ever get married. One girl, just screaming and beating the air, said, "I hate him! I hate him! I hate him!" I just wish I could have reached back in her past and pulled that out and said, "Look, that didn't happen. I got rid of it." What is done is done. Oh, God be thanked that you can be forgiven the guilt of it! You can thank the blood of Jesus for that. Nevertheless, the memory and the consequences of those acts will remain with you for as long as you live. Only heaven itself will erase that memory.

It is not just girls; it is boys too. They are just as guilty in these matters if they engage in them. One boy came in to talk to me because he had made a mistake along this line. I even got out a box of tissues that I keep nearby and started handing them to him across the desk. He and I bowed our heads and prayed in the office that his first mistake would be his last. Not too long ago, another boy came in. He was a virgin. He was engaged to marry a girl, but this girl had confided that she was not a virgin. She would have given anything in the world if she had been, and so would he. He said, "I am having trouble dealing with that." He said, "I don't know if I can accept it or not. Nothing has ever crushed me like that." He said, "I didn't realize it was such a problem until I began to talk about it with other boys; and many, many others have had to wrestle with this same thing." I tried to tell him that he could still marry her, and that one of the very best ways he could confirm his love for her would be to forgive her. This was about two years ago, and that boy is not married yet. I don't know what led to the breakup of that engagement. I never asked, but I have a feeling that I know one of the main factors.

For the sake of that boy or girl you are out with, for the man or the woman that he or she will marry and the woman or the man whom you will marry, keep yourself pure. For your mother and your father, whose hearts tremble for your safety and welfare, and for your children one day whom you will want to teach these same things, and for all of those others who may be affected, keep yourself pure. Girls, you don't owe a boy a kiss for the night. I would give him his quarter back if that is all he is wanting. You don't owe him a thing except "Thank you." Boys, when you kiss that girl good night, that should say to her, "You are special to me. I really, really like you a lot. You are not just ordinary in my book." You know, the trouble is that these acts of affection can also be used in a lustful sense. When we use the embraces and the fondling and the kisses in order to stimulate us, to excite us, and to arouse our passion, that is lust. Do you want to know what lust is? Lust is when you are getting physically aroused. When two people find themselves chemically, biologically, and physically stimulated and what was done last night is not enough for tonight and what was done tonight is not enough for tomorrow night, more has to be done to reach the same peak until a couple finally burns out. That is lust.

Some people think, "As long as we don't go all the way we are okay." That is wrong. It is a sin back there on lust. Young people, have the good sense to break it off, to quit. Start up that car motor; get out of that alley or the cemetery or wherever you are. You didn't think I knew those places, did you? Go down and buy a Coke. Pour it on your head! Go home and read your history book. That will cool anybody off. Get in a crowd. I don't think that most of our young people who get in trouble along this line intended to do so. Of course, you are going to school with a lot of people who use that as their regular nightly entertainment, and you know that. I don't think our Christian young people do that. I think they just keep tempting themselves. A person can tempt himself so long that he loses the power to resist. The point is, young people, don't ever get in a state like that. Have the good sense to stop; pray with each other on dates if you are seriously dating. Help each other set guidelines and hold to those guidelines.

Paul said, "Flee immorality. Every other sin that a man commits is outside the body, but the immoral man sins against his own body" (1 Corinthians 6:18). The body is the temple of the Holy Spirit. Paul says fornication defiles the body as no other sin does. There is no other sin that defiles the body like fornication. In Genesis 39:12, Potiphar's wife grabbed Joseph and said, "Lie with me!" and he wouldn't do it. She took hold of his coat, and he shed that coat and ran outside. He fled temptation. The bravest thing you can do sometimes is to run. Fight it with your feet. Pick them up and put them down as hard as you can. Now, Joseph could have said to Potiphar's wife, "You had better give me my coat back." She would have said, "Come and get it." He donated one coat to the cause, didn't he? He got out of the situation. He got out of the house completely. He realized that he, as a young, normal Hebrew male, could yield to that temptation if he allowed himself to go that far.

Winston Churchill, in encouraging the people in the dark days of World War II, closed one of his speeches by saying, "Never give in. Never give in. Never, never, never, never." I would like to say that same thing to you, young people. Never give in. Never give in. Never, never, never. I think the whole key is back in Genesis 39:9. When Joseph was talking to Potiphar's wife, he said, ". . . How then could I do this great evil and sin against God?" Young people, you don't have it all together until you behave as you should because of your relationship with God. It is not enough for you to behave because Mama and Daddy will punish you if they find out or the preacher will embarrass you. That is not enough. Somewhere or other there has to be a governor within each of you, a personal accountability to God.

Some young people live by only one commandment: "Thou shalt not get caught." They think that if they don't get caught, it is all right. "I cheated on that test, and they never knew it. The teacher never knew it, never even saw it." There is a God in heaven who saw it, and I would just faint from embarrassment if He stood in front of me and told me that He had seen me commit some sin. "I was out last night with so-and-so, and what we did nobody will ever know." There is a God in heaven who saw it. "I took that money the other day. Nobody saw me do it. I got away with it." There is a God in heaven who saw it. You can go on and make other applications of it, can't you? Young people, you are not ready to go out and live a life of commitment to the Lord until you have that personal commitment with the Lord Jesus Christ. When you have that commitment, we can trust you out on any date with anybody in any situation.

I told my children many times, "It is not enough for you to act like that because you are a preacher's kid. Don't say that. It is not enough for you to act right because you are afraid we are going to find out. Our job with you is not finished until you live right because your relationship with the Lord Jesus Christ is right. When you have that personal relationship with the Lord right, it doesn't matter who is around, who sees you, who hears you, or if no one does. You have a faith that will get you to heaven."

TEN COMMANDMENTS FOR YOUTH #2

QUESTIONS

1. What does 1 Samuel 16:7 teach?

2. Acting in what three ways will gain the trust of your parents?

3. How are young people going to gain more privileges?

4. What is one of the best ways you can influence non-Christians?

5. What is true about young people that cannot be over-impressed (Matthew 5:14–16)?

6. Why should we choose our close friends carefully?

7. While we are to choose our close friends carefully, should that affect those with whom we associate?

8. When does all the shame and the stigma surrounding sex occur?

9. What is lust?

5
So You Want to Get Married

> *Do not be bound together with unbelievers; for what partnership have righteousness and lawlessness, or what fellowship has light with darkness? Or what harmony has Christ with Belial, or what has a believer in common with an unbeliever? (2 Corinthians 6:14, 15).*

Whenever I am asked to speak to young people, if they don't assign me a subject, this is the sermon they get. Whenever they do assign me a subject, if I can talk them out of it, this is the sermon they get. This is my favorite sermon to preach to young people—not because it is the only one I have, but because I think it is the most important subject that could possibly be spoken to young people.

I was told one time that a couple came to church right before Sunday school and wanted the preacher to preach the wedding for them. He said, "We are about to have Sunday school and church; but if you will sit through the Sunday school and church, I will be glad to oblige you when the church service is over." They patiently sat through Sunday school and church. Right at the end of the service, before the closing prayer, he said, "After prayer, those wishing to get married please come forward, and I will be glad to visit with you." At the conclusion of the prayer, one man and thirty-seven women came forward!

I don't expect that type of response today, but I do want to talk on this subject: "So You Want to Get Married." I want to divide the lesson into three points, and they all start with the letter "P."

THE PLAN

The first "P" is God's plan for marriage. The one thing I want to stress in this point is that God's plan is that marriage is for keeps. Do you know what "keeps" is? When I was in the first or second grade, a little buddy went home with me from school to play marbles. We were over at the house playing marbles; and he said, "Do you want to play for keeps?" I didn't know what "keeps" was, but I didn't want him to think I was dumb. I said, "Sure, keeps." So we played a little while; and an hour later he said, "I'm going home." I said, "Come on. Stay with me a little longer. Let's play some more." He said, "You don't have any more marbles." I said, "Of course I do. All of these marbles are mine." He said, "Oh, no, we played for keeps; and they are mine." He took my marbles home with him. That is the first time I learned what playing for "keeps" meant. It is also the first time I lost my marbles.

Marriage is for keeps. It is not like trading in a car if you don't like the one you have. That is not the way it is. The one thing the Bible teaches is that marriage is for as long as you both shall live.

Turn with me to Matthew 19, where you see the threefold stage of God's plan for marriage: first, the way God planned it at the beginning; second, the way God tolerated it during the Old Testament days; and third, our Lord's statement which is applicable to you and me:

> Some Pharisees came to Jesus, testing Him and asking, "Is it lawful for a man to divorce his wife for any reason at all?" And He answered and said, "Have you not read that He who created them from the beginning made them male and female, and said, 'For this reason a man shall leave his father and mother and be joined to his wife, and the two shall become one flesh'? So they are no longer two but one flesh. What therefore God has joined

together, let no man separate" (Matthew 19:3–6).

Our Lord, first of all, took the people back to the way it was in the very beginning. When God saw that Adam needed a wife, He made one woman for him and that was it. He brought Eve to Adam and said, "Now choose a wife." That was about the only choice he had, either Eve or a giraffe. Maybe you heard the story about Adam and Eve in the garden; and Eve said, "Adam, do you love me?" All wives ask that every now and then. He looked around the garden, and then he looked at her. He said, "Pray tell me, who else?" He didn't have any choice to love anyone else, did he? The only choice he had was to take it or leave it. Our Lord says God intended a lesson right there: one man and one woman for life. Here in Matthew 19:5, we have a quotation from Genesis 2:24: "For this reason a man shall leave his father and mother, and be joined to his wife; and the two shall become one flesh." This is the way God planned it at the beginning.

Stage two is the way man began to tamper with God's plan. We have, first of all, polygamy coming in. So we have deviations from God's plan of one man and one woman. I would really be impressed if any of you knew who was the first man to have more than one wife. It is a man in Genesis 4 named Lamech, a descendant of Cain. He had two wives named Adah and Zillah. That ought to be something to stump your teacher with when you get back to Sunday school. Later, Abraham had Sarah and Hagar. Jacob had Leah and Rachel. The ultimate in polygamy would have been Solomon. He had a thousand wives.

Not only did they practice such plurality of marriages, but they also indulged in divorce. Matthew 19:7 says, "They said to Him, 'Why then did Moses command to give her a certificate of divorce and send her away?'" They were thinking about Deuteronomy 24:1–3. The law of divorce in the Old Testament is in Deuteronomy 24:1 and following. The Lord said there that if a man puts away his wife and she becomes the wife of another man, there is no way the first man can ever take her back. Even if the second husband dies, he can never take her back. In other words, when you let your wife go, you had better make sure you don't ever want to have her back again. "Why was this permitted?" the Jews asked. Matthew 19:8 says, "He said to them, 'Because of your hardness of heart Moses permitted you to divorce your wives; but from the beginning it has not been this way.'" It looks as if Jesus was saying, "You were not morally mature enough as people to live according to God's strict ordinance." God tolerated this, at least, for the time being; and that is stage two.

Now, if you are going to go to sleep or tune me out, you had better not do it right now. This is the most important thing I am going to say. If I were at school, I would say, "This is going to be on a test." That wakes everybody up. I've seen them come to life and grab their pencils. This is going to be on a test—not on a written test, but on a living test. If you are going to forget anything, don't forget this. If you are going to remember anything, remember this. Stage three is what did our Lord say for you and me? Matthew 19:9 says, "And I say to you, whoever divorces his wife, except for immorality, and marries another woman commits adultery." Our Lord restated the way it was in the beginning and gave one exception: That is, if your partner is guilty of fornication, you have the right to put him or her away. Fornication, in case you want me to spell it out for you, is extramarital sex. It can be homosexual acts; it can be premarital sex; it can be adultery, which is between married people who are not married to each other. He was saying here that sexual unfaithfulness is the only thing that gives a person the privilege or the right to put away a wife or a husband and marry again.

The Bible doesn't say you have to put the unfaithful one away. I believe you should stay with the marriage nearly every time you possibly can. Work it out. Stay together. If your partner has committed fornication and the situation is irreconcilable, then you have the scriptural right to divorce and remarry. If your wife lies, steals, and cheats, you still can't marry again. If she drinks, if she eats crackers in bed, you still can't marry again. You might want to get twin beds. If she is a murderess, you can't marry again. You may want to move before she poisons you. You may want to eat out for a while, but you can't marry again. There are provisions in other places for a possible separation and instances where maybe these would be advised, such as when a partner is being abused. The right to remarry is found only if the person is guilty of fornication.

People can get in messes that even Solomon could not have straightened out. Someone might say, "What am I going to do? I've got four husbands. My second one and I had three kids, I had four by the third one, and two by the first one, and six by the fourth one. What am I going to do?" I don't know what that person could do. Young people, you are not in that mess, are you? There is no excuse for any one of you getting in that mess. That is why I came here today to keep you from getting in a mess like that. Don't come to me years from now saying, "What am I going to do? I have four husbands and twelve kids." I am going to say, "Get out of here." I am going to say, "I told you not to do that. Shame on you." No, I can't straighten out all of them. Personally, if I or my wife either one did not have a scriptural divorce and right to marry, I don't believe I could live together with her. I would have to live a life of celibacy. Personally, I believe that is the answer. That is the safe way—but I am not going to stand here as the know-it-all on this subject.

Not long ago, a girl called me from Mississippi and said, "I am so-and-so. I was in your Bible class. Do you remember me?" I tried hard to remember her. I thought I did. She said, "I am engaged to this young man, and I want you to tell me if you think we can get married." I said, "Maybe I can tell you. Is he a Christian?" "Oh, yes, we met at church," she said. Then I asked, "Has he been married before?" She got quiet for a little bit and said, "Yes, he has." I said, "Does he have a scriptural divorce?" I didn't have to tell her what one was. She knew. Then she got very quiet. She said, "No, he doesn't." I said, "Then, you can't marry him." She paused a minute and said, "I just knew you would say that! I just knew you would say that!" If you are going to call me and ask me this, I will save you your time. No, you can't do it.

I got another call from one of my former students who said, "I can't get the preacher here to perform my wedding ceremony. Am I going to have to get a Justice of the Peace in order to marry this fellow?" I said, "What is wrong? Has he been married before?" She said, "Yes." I said, "Does he have a scriptural divorce?" She said, "No." I said, "I don't think you ought to marry him. I don't think you should get a Justice of the Peace or anybody else." It is just as simple as that. No, you can't do it. I wish I could tell everybody that everything is fine; just go out and marry whomever you want to. However, my job is to teach and preach the Word of God. This is what the Lord Jesus Christ said, and I have no right to add to it or take from it: "Whoever divorces his wife, except for immorality, and marries another commits adultery."

THE PERSON

The second "P" is the person whom you should marry. In four different ways, I want to impress upon you as you have never had impressed upon you before that Christians should marry Christians. I mean that members of the church should marry members of the church. I have four reasons for that, and any one of them is enough to stand by itself.

Reason number one is for the sake of the Scriptures themselves. In Deuteronomy 7, Moses was preparing the children of Israel to enter the Promised Land. He said, "Don't have a thing to do with those Canaanites in that land. You tear down their altars, and you burn their idols." Then in Deuteronomy 7:3, 4, he said,

> Furthermore, you shall not intermarry with them; you shall not give your daughters to their sons, nor shall you take their daughters for your sons. For they will turn your sons away from following Me to serve other gods. . . .

For a long time, I thought that God did not want Jews to marry people of another race or nation. The main thing God wanted was for them not to marry people of another religion. He said, "If you marry these people, they will turn your heart away from your God."

If you want a classic example of that, turn to 1 Kings 11. Verses 1 and 2 say,

> Now King Solomon loved many foreign women along with the daughter of Pharaoh: Moabite, Ammonite, Edomite, Sidonian, and Hittite women, from the nations concerning which the Lord had said to the sons of Israel, "You shall not associate with them, nor shall they associate with you, for they will surely turn your heart away after their gods." Solomon held fast to these in love.

Solomon went after the gods of these women. When he was old, his wives turned away his heart after other gods. This was the sin that led to the division of the kingdom. Ten tribes went north; two tribes went south. The kingdom was split in two and stayed that way. Do you know what sin basically caused it? It was Solomon's sin in marrying these women. It is ironic that the smartest, the wisest man in the world did one of the dumbest things anybody could do. That is exactly what happened.

I know what some of you are thinking: "That is the Old Testament. Can you give me something out of the New Testament?" I am so glad you asked. Come to 1 Corinthians 7. Paul, in verse 39, was talking about widows, Christian widows! "A wife is bound as long as her husband lives; but if her husband is dead, she is free to be married to whom she wishes...." Are you ready for this? "... only in the Lord." Among other things, I believe that means to marry a Christian. Some of you are saying, "What about the first time? This is the second marriage." With the first marriage, she probably was not a Christian. Besides that, do you know who usually arranged those first marriages? Mama and Daddy. Aren't you glad that doesn't work today? Wouldn't that be awful? She didn't have much choice about whom to marry the first time. Now, in this particular framework, she had the freedom to choose; and Paul said to marry only in the Lord.

Let me give you another one while you are listening: 1 Corinthians 9:5. It says, "Do we not have a right to take along a believing wife, even as the rest of the apostles and the brothers of the Lord and Cephas?" Paul said, "I have the right to get married." He was an old bachelor. Did you notice whom he gave himself the right to marry? He said, "I have the right to marry a sister." Do you want to guess what a "sister" is? A "sister" is a believer. Some of you probably have Bibles that say "a wife who is a believer." Paul didn't even think about marrying someone who wasn't a Christian. He said, in effect, "The brethren of the Lord married Christians. Peter married a Christian. The other apostles married Christians." It looks to me as if you and I should marry Christians. Doesn't that look like the normal conclusion?

Can you imagine Paul marrying somebody who wasn't a Christian? I can't. Can't you just see someone saying, "Where is Mrs. Paul today? Why isn't she at the services?" and someone answering, "Oh, she took the kids over to the Baal temple today. They had the sacrifice and the orgy today, and she doesn't want to miss that every year." Imagine the church elders wanting him to come and preach in a meeting; and Paul saying, "I can't that week because the wife goes to the Diana temple and they have the big Easter egg roll event up there. I really can't leave the kids here alone." That sounds ridiculous, doesn't it? At any rate, Paul said, "I have the right to marry someone who is a Christian"; and he left it at that.

Honestly, I can't understand how a Christian and a non-Christian could be so compatible that they would fall in love, get engaged, and get married. It seems to me as if you were really as committed to the Lord as you should be, you would have so many fusses and squabbles and fights that you never would get along with a non-Christian. It looks to me as if you would be so different in the way you are living and the way you think that there is no way in the world you could be compatible. That is just my personal opinion.

Let me show you another one, though. Second Corinthians 6:14, 15 says, "Do not be bound together with unbelievers; for what partnership have righteousness and lawlessness, or what fellowship has light with darkness? Or what harmony has Christ with Belial, or what has a believer in common with an unbeliever?" I have heard some say, "That means not to be unequally yoked with them. You can be equally yoked, but you can't be unequally yoked." Now, come on. He was saying, "Don't be mismatched with unbelievers." Any yoking with an unbeliever is a mismatch. I have heard some say, "It doesn't say anything about marriage." I ask, "What is it talking about then?" "Well, it is talking about business deals," they say. That is the answer you usually get on this one, isn't it? I don't see business deals in here either, do you? I see a general principle of yoking. Don't be yoked with unbelievers. If there is any yoking in this world, it is being married. Isn't that right? Amen. Ask those who know. Paul was saying, "Don't get in entanglements like that." Someone might say, "Yes, but Paul in 1 Corinthians 7 said to stay married with an unbeliever." I know that. Paul was dealing with a situation where a believer and an unbeliever were married, and one of them has become a Christian in the marriage. He said, "Stay with that person. Maybe you can win him [or her] over." In this context, we are dealing with a situation in which you have the freedom to choose. You are a Christian already. Now you are going to choose a mate. What kind of mate should you choose? Paul said you should choose a Christian.

I feel so strongly about this that I refuse to perform a marriage ceremony between a Christian and a non-Christian. I believe it is wrong. It wasn't too many years ago a friend of ours called me and wanted me to preach her wedding for her. I didn't know the man. I said, "Is he a Christian?" She said, "No, he is not." I said, "Well, I'm sorry. I can't perform the wedding. I know you will probably get married anyway, but I do not believe that you as a Christian girl should marry this man. I cannot condone what you are doing, and I will not be a part of it." That may sound a little harsh to you; but I believe that if marrying outside the church is not a sin, it is the dumbest thing you can do. I honestly believe that. For the sake of the Scriptures themselves, marry a Christian.

Reason number two is for the sake of your soul. I heard a man speak in chapel when I was a student at Harding many years ago. He said when he was courting the girls and would find a good prospect, he would pray, "God, help me to have her if she would help me to go to heaven." How do you like that? I told this to one of my classes; and some boy in the class said, "Let me tell you something better than that. Pray to God, 'Help me have her if it would help us both to go to heaven.'" I believe that is even better.

Young people, it will be hard for you to be faithful to the Lord all of your life, even with the encouragement that is around you. You need a partner in life who will encourage you to do what is right, to be faithful. You not only need a Christian, but you also need someone with the same degree of commitment to the Lord that you have. I would hate to be married to somebody I had to keep dragging to church all the time, someone I had to keep picking at and keep nagging at to do what is right. I need a wife who says, "Get out of that bed and get ready. We are going to serve the Lord today." I need a wife who says, "Get ready. We are going to church. I don't care if you are tired this Wednesday night. We are going to worship the Lord." I need a wife who encourages me. You need a wife like that. You need a husband like that.

One thing that aggravates me about as much as anything is these sweet girls at Harding who find the sorriest boys they can, think they are in love with them, and set out trying to reform them and marry them. I guess it is the mother instinct in girls. Is that what it is? A girl came to talk with me several years ago. Her name was "Sandy." I had known her ever since she was a little girl. In fact, I had preached where she went to church when I was a student. She said, "I am going with this boy back home. He is not a Christian. He has had a hard life." (They have all had hard lives.) When they start, I can almost finish the story for them. "He goes with me to church on Sunday night sometimes. He's not drinking like he used to. Do you have any Scriptures I could use on him? We are going to get married this summer." She had her Bible and her paper and pencil there.

I just chunked everything I had learned about counseling, reared back in my seat, and said, "You need that fellow like you need a hole in the head." I believe in the subtle approach, don't you? I said, "You have gone back home and found the sorriest thing there, probably, and think that he is the one you are going to marry when you have literally hundreds of dedicated Christian boys right here on this campus." She said, "But I think I can help him." I said, "You are so much in love you couldn't help anybody. You can't even see straight, much less help anyone. If you want to be a missionary and straighten out sorry boys, go to it. There are plenty to work on. When you are looking for a husband, don't look for sorry boys. You are looking in the wrong place." She left, and I didn't know whether or not she would ever come back again. That was in the fall semester. In the spring semester, she came back knocking on the door. She had her roommate, "Sharon," with her. I opened the door, invited them in, and told them to sit down. She said, "Sharon is about to marry a boy who is not a Christian. Will you give her the same speech you gave me?" We sat down and talked to Sharon. Then Sandy said, "I have been telling her that, but she won't listen to me." We really worked on Sharon. Sharon left and never came back.

Several years later, I was in a meeting in Rolla, Missouri, I think. Who walked in the church door but Sandy and her husband—who was a Christian, by the way. She had broken up with that other fellow and married a Christian. I said, "Sandy, while we are here, tell me about Sharon. What happened to her?" She said, "Oh, she married a Christian." Two out of two! I don't do that well very often. Two out of two! I am proud of that. Two Christian homes. Christians who married Christians.

I read this in a church bulletin, so I know it is true. Of 49 Christians who marry outside the church, 28 of them will leave the church. Only 21 will remain faithful. That is less than half. Of course, the fact that they married non-Christians shows their spiritual interest was not too high, and the church may have lost half of them regardless of whom they married. Of the 21 who remain faithful, 12 will go to church by themselves all their lives and try to rear their children in the faith by themselves, with no encouragement. Only 9 of the original 49 will ever convert their partners and have Christian homes. That is less than 1 in 5. Some of you are thinking, "My mama converted my daddy" or "My daddy converted my mama." Is that true of anyone you know? For every 1 who converts a spouse, there are 4 who do not.

Suppose you were out by my house and there was a big field there beside it. You say, "The field looks sort of snaky out there." I say, "Yes, there are rattlesnakes out there, but only 4 out of 5 people who go out there get bitten." Would you go across it? Suppose I said 1 out of 5 gets bitten. Would you go across it? Suppose I said one got bitten last year. Would you go across it? I am talking to you about something far more important than a rattlesnake bite. I am talking to you about a soul, about a Christian home. If you marry outside the church, the odds are less than 20 percent that you will ever have a

Christian home. If that boy you marry is a non-Christian, you are cutting the odds to less than 20 percent that your children will ever have a Christian father.

I went back to a place where I had preached when I was in graduate school and held a gospel meeting. I wanted to check on the young people in the church. They were already grown and married and had families of their own. I wanted to see how many of them were faithful. We had had wiener roasts, skating parties, youth rallies, and teenage classes. We had really done it right. With one exception, every one of those young people who had married Christians was faithful to the Lord, and every one of them who had married outside the Lord was unfaithful. One elder's daughter had married outside the Lord and was still faithful; but, eighteen years later, she still had a husband who was not a believer. She had reared her children without a Christian father. I thought, "Maybe I should have forgotten about all these other things and taught on the importance of marrying Christians." I realize other factors enter in besides the marriage partner, but I am firmly convinced that this is one of the most important. For the sake of your soul, marry a Christian.

Number three is for the sake of your home. Wouldn't you love to be married to somebody who fusses and complains every time you go to church? Wouldn't you love to be married to somebody who resents the time and the money you give to the Lord, who doesn't like the friends you have because they are Christians? I have never known of anyone to marry outside the church who recommended that other people do it. I have never known of anyone to marry outside the church to tell me, "My home is happier than if we both were Christians." I have issued that challenge many times and have never had a taker.

Jesus said in John 12:32, "And I, if I am lifted up from the earth, will draw all men to Myself." You have your partner pulling you one way, and the Lord pulling you another way. Something has to give. Your relationship with your partner is going to be strained; your relationship with the Lord is going to be strained. It will be one or the other, or you will be split down the middle. If you find a Christian partner who has the same beliefs and goals in life that you have, then you have something that will hold that home together—and the devil himself can't destroy it. For the sake of your home, marry a Christian.

Number four and final, can you guess what this one will be? When I was preaching in Illinois, I got a phone call about ten o'clock one night. One of the fellows who went to church where I preached was on the phone. He said, "You have to help us. My wife goes to her church; I go to where you are preaching. We have three kids. The oldest one is about ten years old. We can't keep dragging them back and forth. What are we going to do?" I felt like saying, "It is a fine time for you to think about that," and hang up on him. Being the sweet fellow I am, I didn't do that. It struck me as odd that he would be married twelve years before he thought of what a foolish thing he had done. It looks as if he would have thought of that about eleven years before, at least.

Have you figured out what the fourth point is yet? Let me give you another clue. I was out playing with my little buddy Phil. We were about nine or ten years old, and one Saturday afternoon we were sitting on the curb visiting. All of a sudden, he just grabbed his head and said, "Oh, no, tomorrow is Sunday. I hate Sundays." I never hated Sunday. Monday was the bad one for me. I said, "What is wrong with Sunday? We can play all afternoon." He said, "It is terrible at my house on Sunday. Mama says, 'Go to church with me,' and Daddy says, 'Go to church with me.' Daddy starts yelling, and Mama starts crying. I hate Sundays." Have you figured out point number four yet?

Number four is for the sake of your children. Your children don't have any choice about the parents they get. They have no say at all about whether or not they are brought up in a Christian home, but you do. The greatest gift you could bestow on your children is not a great inheritance or even an education, for that matter. The greatest gift you could bestow on them would be a Christian home. The greatest thing you girls could give your children would be a Christian father. The greatest thing you boys could ever give your children would be a Christian mother. You have the right to choose that.

Girls, you had better back off and look at that fellow you are thinking about. He may be the greatest sweetheart in the world and the most wonderful thing you have ever seen on two legs. He may be able to run the 100-yard dash in 9.0, and he may be able to dunk the basketball and do all these other things that seem so important. I will tell you one thing, though: You had better look at him again if he is going to be the father of your children. All of a sudden, these other things don't look very important, do they? Boys, that girl just may be the sweetest sweetheart and just send your heart aflutter as she flutters those eyelashes, even if they are false. She may be the sweetest thing in the world to you and the ultimate of your dreams. You had better back off and look at her again because, if you marry her, she is going to be the mother of your children. What kind of mother do you want your children to have?

My children have a Christian mother. It is really a comforting thought that while I am gone they are going to be at church, that when they eat they are going to pray, and before they go to bed they are going to pray to God. Whatever comes up will be dealt with from the biblical standpoint. That is a big, nice, warm feeling down in my tummy. Do you know why my children have a Christian mother? I bet you never could guess. Go ahead and try. I married a Christian. It is so obvious, you would think somebody else would think of it, wouldn't you? You would think it would be so obvious that everyone would want to do it. I married a Christian. Long after the beauty trophies that she has sitting there on the shelf and her basketball trophies that she shines up every now and then and whatever else she has around there to remind her of younger days and glories pretty well fade out, do you know what really shines in that woman to me today? She is a Christian. She loves the Lord, and she has trained our children to love the Lord. The greatest thing I have ever given my children is a Christian home, and that happened because I married a Christian.

THE PREPARATION

The third "P" is preparation for marriage. I have three things to say to you. *Number one is this: Don't get in a hurry to get married.* A girl about sixteen years old realizes she doesn't have a steady boyfriend. It makes her so nervous. She thinks, "Everybody else is going steady. I am going to be an old maid." Then she gets out of high school. Everybody in the class gets married except her, and there is nothing left for her to do but go to Harding or some other Christian school. Then she goes through college in about four years and really hits the panic button when she graduates and still nothing is in sight. Don't get in a hurry to get married. Anybody can get married. That is no big deal. Marrying the right person—that is a big deal. Being married to the wrong person is a whole lot worse than not being married at all.

The reason so many teenage marriages don't last is that people grow up after they get married and find out they don't even like each other and are not even compatible. Young people, don't get married now. You can do better a little later. You are getting prettier, more handsome, more mature, wiser, suaver, and more debonair. You can do better when you are twenty-one than when you are sixteen or eighteen. Wait until you go down the other side and then grab a husband. I said that one time and one girl came up and said, "I am already down the other side. What do I do now?" Start back up, I guess. I don't know. Don't get in a hurry to get married. This is the second most important decision you will ever make, second only to your decision to be a Christian. It could well affect your faithfulness to that most important decision.

Suggestion number two is this: You have to go where Christians are if you are going to get a good Christian mate. It is just like fishing.

It doesn't matter how great a fisherman you are and how expensive your equipment is. If you fish in a bathtub, you will never catch anything because there is nothing in there. You have to go where they are. A girl wrote Ann Landers one time and said, "Why is it that every man I meet down at the bar turns out to be no good?" Go to Christian camps. Go to youth meetings. Go to services. My mother told me a long time ago, "When you go to a strange place, choose your friends from the Wednesday night crowd at church." You don't have to check out everybody in town. Those who would not be good companions will weed themselves out automatically. Just see who shows up at a midweek Bible study. They are the ones who are really interested in what should interest you.

When I was in high school, I thought there must not have been more than three or four good Christian girls. There were two where I went to church. One of them didn't want me, and I didn't want the other one. That pretty well took care of that. Then I went to Freed-Hardeman College; and I felt like the little boy who fell into a barrel of molasses and said, "Lord, make me equal to the opportunity that lies before me." I had never seen so many Christian girls, all there just ready to be asked out, ready to form a relationship. Go to a Christian school. Go where they are.

We parents can't determine whom our children will marry, but we surely can stack the odds in our favor. We can put our children on a Christian campus where about 90 percent of their classmates will be Christians.

Third, you must be the right kind to catch the right kind. Again, finding a mate is a lot like fishing. By the bait you drop in the water, you attract certain fish and repel other fish. Girls, by the way you dress or don't dress, by the way you talk, by the places you go, by the people you associate with, by the things you engage in or don't engage in, you are attracting certain ones of the opposite sex. They are saying, "That is my kind of person." You are repelling the others. If you are a loose girl, certain boys will beat a path to your door—but who wants any of them? If you are an outstanding Christian girl who dresses and talks and behaves in a decent manner and keeps herself pure and holy in God's sight and is a good influence on others, there are good, decent Christian boys who are looking for you and would give anything they have to find a girl like you. They are the ones worth finding. Boys, there are good Christian girls there, but they will not give you a second look until you shape up and until you have advertised by the way you look, by the way you talk, by the way you dress, by your interests, and by your love for the Lord that this is what you are really serious about. You have to be the right kind to attract the right kind.

Conclusion

Young people, don't trade your soul for a husband or a wife. Don't lose your head. Put first things first. You may hear better lessons than this, better organized, shorter, more scholarly, more eloquently delivered, or whatever else you want to say. I can promise you one thing, though: You will never hear a more important lesson than this one at your stage in life when you are looking forward to marriage. I am convinced of that.

May God help you live up to that commitment, and may God give you the wisdom to make that decision. Pray to God, and give Him the opportunity to guide you to that one who can lead you to heaven and bring your family to the Lord. When you come right down to it, that is all there is in life anyway.

QUESTIONS

1. What is God's plan for marriage?

2. How did man begin to tamper with God's plan?

3. What did the law of Moses in Deuteronomy 24 say concerning marriage?

4. What did our Lord say in the New Testament concerning marriage (Matthew 19)?

5. Why was divorce permitted by Moses?

6. What are four reasons that Christians should marry Christians?

7. What three suggestions are given concerning preparation for marriage?

6
Happily Ever After

"And I, if I am lifted up from the earth, will draw all men to Myself" (John 12:32).

"And they lived happily ever after": We do not read this in newspapers or biographies. The only place we read this statement is in fairy tales, and that is probably the only place it belongs.

One of the most important needs in the church—and, for that matter, the world—is happy homes. A marriage ceremony does not give people a happy home. It only gives them a legal right to try to build a happy home. It takes a great deal of hard work, sacrifice, and patience to make a home what it ought to be. Here are five R's that comprise a recipe for a happy home.

1. RAPPORT

"Rapport" means communicating with one another. It indicates that one not only is understanding what the other is saying but also has a spirit of empathy with that person. Any home that has a communication problem will have a problem in relationships.

Be available. As husbands and wives, we have to *make* time to be with each other. When God said it was not good for man to be alone, He meant after marriage as well as before marriage. We cannot have quality time unless we invest some quantity.

It is hard to schedule quality time. A man cannot just tell his wife, "From 10:15 to 10:25 this evening, we will have quality time." Quality time comes after we have been together, worked together, and maybe even argued together. It seems that in these very special moments we really can communicate.

Be interested in the other's interests. A husband and a wife should be interested in what the other is saying and thinking. A husband should communicate with his wife that he really cares about what she is saying. The exhortation of James 1:19 certainly fits in a home situation: "But everyone must be quick to hear, slow to speak and slow to anger."

Be open. For effective communication, we must be able to speak freely about what is bothering us, especially if it is hurting our relationship. Jesus' exhortation in Matthew 18:15 for the offended party to go to the offender certainly applies in a home situation. This is far better than silently burning with resentment or subtly punishing or seeking revenge against the spouse.

Be willing to resolve differences. In any normal relationship, problems will develop. With two healthy personalities, differences of opinion will inevitably occur. The fact that there are differences is not nearly so important as the way they are resolved.

One man told me that a person needs to marry someone who does not believe in divorce, and then they will both *have* to adjust. The reason many young couples today do not make their marriages work is that they do not put forth the effort necessary to resolve their differences. In the context of a Christian marriage, we promise to stay with one another—and we must be willing to make the necessary sacrifices in order to do that.

I honestly believe that if two people are committed to working out their differences, they will do it. When only one is willing to do it, there is not much hope; but with both committed to problem-solving, there is hardly any problem that cannot be overcome.

2. Respect

A happy marriage must be based on mutual respect. First, the husband should respect his wife. It bothers me when a woman describes herself as "just a housewife." The general opinion seems to be that a woman has to apologize for being "nothing more than" a housewife. If she is not an office manager or a bank executive, then she is led to believe that she is not very important.

I know of no greater honor or position for any woman than that of being a Christian wife and mother. Paul exhorted young widows to marry and rule the household (1 Timothy 5:14). He told the older women to train the younger women to be workers at home (Titus 2:5). We husbands should honor our wives for the good job they do in being wives and mothers.

Likewise, the wife is to respect her husband. Paul told wives in Ephesians 5:22, "Be subject to your own husbands, as to the Lord." The husband is to be the head of the house. Most women would prefer it that way. The home has more order, more peace and harmony, when each person assumes his or her proper role of responsibility.

Of course, some husbands require a better understanding of what it means to be the head of the house. It does not mean ruling as a dictator would. Being the head means that the husband is responsible for the welfare of the family. He is to put their needs and interests before his own. Being the head may mean that he seldom gets his own selfish way. It is his responsibility to look out for the welfare of his family, and it is their responsibility to encourage him in this great work.

In Ephesians 5, wives are never told to love their husbands; but husbands are told three times to love their wives (5:25, 28, 33). Perhaps Paul realized that if husbands would treat their wives as they should, the wives could not keep from loving them.

3. Reserve

Some things ought to be kept to ourselves alone, like our criticisms and our tempers. We must allow the other person in a marriage room to live, to grow, and to be himself or herself. It has been said that an ideal husband is like a shoe that covers the foot but still lets the foot go where it wants to go. A wife should allow her husband the right to live without continual nagging and prodding. It is better when a man does the necessary work around the house on his own initiative, without being reminded by his wife.

Intimate details of a marriage belong to no one but the two of you alone—not even your parents, neighbors, or closest friends. Before my wife and I married, a woman at a worship service met me at the door afterward and said, "Support your wife, even if she is wrong! Never side against your wife on the side of your mother."

We do not love our parents any less when we get married. In fact, we appreciate them more when we have the responsibility of rearing our own children. However, once we have a wife or a husband, our first love must be for that spouse. I believe that every woman has the right to be number one in her husband's heart. I have felt sorry for Leah in the Old Testament because she was always in competition with her sister, Rachel, for the affections of Jacob.

4. Romance

Too many married couples have forgotten why they married one another. You need to tell your husband (or wife) that you love him (or her). I remember one woman at church telling me before I got married that I should tell my wife that I love her three times a day. It is good to be reassured. I heard of one man who said, "When I think of all that my wife does for me and means to me, it is all I can do sometimes to keep from telling her!" I have opportunities twenty-four hours a day to show my wife how much I love her—not only by the words I say, but also by the kind deeds I do.

In the Christian home, there is no place for jealousy, flirtation, or distrust. A meaningful relationship between a husband and a wife has to be built upon a solid foundation of trust. No one else should dare to intrude on that special relationship. My wife must know that I belong to her and to her alone.

5. Religion

Jesus said in John 1:32, "And I, if I be lifted up from the earth, will draw all men to myself." Two people cannot be drawn nearer to Jesus without coming nearer to each other. When a husband and his wife worship together and live in accordance with God's Word together, their relationship and their home will have a security and a solidity that will withstand the trials and the pressures of this life.

Questions

1. What is the meaning of the word "rapport"?

2. How can couples achieve effective communication?

3. On what must a happy marriage be based?

4. What does being the head of the house mean?

5. What becomes true if both the husband and the wife are drawing nearer to Christ?

7
God's Plan for Marriage

Marriage is to be held in honor among all, and the marriage bed is to be undefiled; for fornicators and adulterers God will judge (Hebrews 13:4).

I want us to look at the Christian view of sex. The first really important thing I want you to learn is that the Bible does not treat sex as a dirty, filthy subject. The Bible treats sex as what it should be, which is something nice, decent, and proper in its right place.

HIS PLAN FOR THE MARRIED

God made man and put him in the garden of Eden with the flowers, the trees, the shrubs, and the vegetables. It was a perfect paradise, but God said it was not good for a man to be alone. God said that He would make a helper for him, so He made woman (Genesis 2:18, 22).

The Hebrew word for "suitable" in Genesis 2:18 is an interesting word. It is an adjective that means "fitting to" or "suiting to." The idea conveyed is that of a matched set. If you take an apple and cut it in two, one half matches the other half. It is not complete without both halves.

God made sex right then. He could have made another man as a companion for Adam. He could have said, "Adam, I want you to meet Henry"—but He did not. He said, "I want you to meet Eve." The Lord could have made them just alike, but aren't you glad that He didn't? Isn't it wonderful that we can have this type of relationship?

God created the organs in our bodies and put those hormones in our bloodstreams. They are part of His plan. No shame at all was connected with God's creation. The first shame came when sin entered the world with the eating of the forbidden fruit. God, at the beginning, made everything pure and holy.

Song of Solomon has given Bible critics a hard time. They really cannot reconcile how such an earthly book can be in the Old Testament. It is a love poem. It tells of Solomon's love for his wife. Chapter 4 describes the beauty of a woman, starting at her head and moving down. Chapter 6 is where the woman describes the beauty of the man. Chapter 7 describes the beauty of the woman again.

I do not see why we have to explain it away. Some people say that it is an allegory of God's love for Israel or Christ's love for the church, but it is a song memorializing a man and a woman in a love relationship. The song has one thing to say to us. This relationship can be beautiful and wonderful.

From the biblical viewpoint, nothing is shameful about the attraction of one sex to another. The desire for sex is a normal physical appetite, like hunger. Some of you get hungry three times a day. Some of you get up hungry and go to bed hungry. You do not feel guilty about having that appetite, but the appetite can be abused by gluttony or drunkenness. Those things are sins because the normal, healthy appetite has been violated. The same thing is true of the sexual appetite.

God has not filled your body with desires that you must repress for the rest of your life. He did not create passions that can so easily be aroused and provide no outlet for them. Rather, He has given us a way in which these desires can be beautifully and completely satisfied—and that is within the realm of marriage. In marriage, God has given us a place where all of these pent-up cravings can be released. During the period of waiting for that time, one of the greatest problems you must confront is fleshly temptation. With God's help and the right attitude, you can manage it.

In 1 Corinthians 7:3, 4, Paul said,

> The husband must fulfill his duty to his wife, and likewise also the wife to her husband. The wife does not have authority over her own body, but the husband does; and likewise also the husband does not have authority over his own body, but the wife does.

In Hebrews 13:4, we read, "Marriage is to be held in honor among all, and the marriage bed is to be undefiled." The marriage relationship is pure. God has no complaint at all about it.

The next big thing that I want you to notice is that all of the sin, shame, and problems come from an abuse of God's principles. The sin of homosexuality is one example. People can call it what they want to in our society, but the Bible identifies it as a sin. The Old Testament called for a death penalty for those who committed that sin. Incest is likewise condemned in the Old Testament. These things are wrong. They are sins. That is where the shame and problems come in.

When God made mankind, He made one man and one woman. That is the way He planned it. God did not even give him the opportunity to look at another woman. His only choice was to accept Eve or reject her.

People can get into messes that even Paul, in all his wisdom, could not have straightened out. You know what the Bible says on the matter: You are not to leave your partner until death, unless that person is guilty of fornication.

God knows what is best for us. It amazes me. I remember a man who came up to me one time and said, "You know when I first became a Christian, I didn't think God knew what He was doing, running a church by elders. But now that I have been here a while, I know He knew what He was talking about.

It works best that way."

God also knew what He was doing when He gave His plan for marriage to men and women. It works best that way. It is best for you. That is why God gave every law in His book—because it is best for you. At times, polygamy was tolerated, but did the wives get along?

I remember hearing a talk one time, and the speaker said, "I feel sorry for Solomon and all of those wives he had." I thought to myself that I had never felt sorry for Solomon. He said, "What kind of meaningful relationship could he have had with one thousand women? One woman is enough for any man!"

If you want to find people who know the real meaning of love, physical as well as spiritual, then find a man and a woman who have lived together, shared their lives together, worked together, fought together, laughed together, cried together, and given themselves completely to one another through the years. That union cannot be surpassed.

We can look around and see the problems that have developed because people have not followed God's law. We do not even need a Scripture to show how foolish such a course of action can be. We see the tensions in the home, the divorce rate, unhappy children, and unwanted children. We see that God knew what He was doing when He created man and woman and marriage. What God has joined together, let man not separate.

HIS PLAN FOR THE UNMARRIED

Application should also be made to those who are not married. Not only is the breaking of a marriage bond a violation of God's principle, but premarital sex is likewise a violation. Nowadays, young people are bombarded with the idea that it is all right, that nothing is wrong with it. The philosophy of "If it feels right, do it" is not in the Word of God. The Bible teaches that sexual intimacy is to be reserved for marriage.

God's laws were given for your benefit. Nothing is more wonderful than to approach the marriage altar wearing white. Nothing is more beautiful than saving yourself for the one who can mean the most to you and the wonderful knowledge that you have something special to give that person as a wedding present. That is where real meaning comes from.

Young men and women have talked to me about the problems caused by premarital sex. They have sat in my office with tears streaming down their faces until my heart ached for them.

God's commands apply both to boys and to girls. You can be forgiven of the guilt of breaking these commands. The blood of Jesus can wash anything away. No sin is beyond His reach. Even so, you will always have a memory of these things. Time and again, throughout your life, you will face the consequences of the mistakes you have made. Whatever you may call it, the Bible calls it "fornication."

Ironically, girls who get caught or become pregnant may be the fortunate ones. They are usually the ones who are brought to repentance. More tragic than their experiences are the consequences for the individuals who continue to sin. Their sins are never found out, and so they persist in their sinful lifestyle. They are headed only one direction.

I want to offer some practical advice on how to avoid such a pitfall. The place to begin is at the cause of the trouble, which is lust. Our Lord said in Matthew 5:27, 28,

> You have heard that it was said, "You shall not commit adultery"; but I say to you that everyone who looks at a woman with lust for her has already committed adultery with her in his heart.

Admiring physical beauty is different from allowing oneself to be engrossed in the sin of lust. We need to remember the purpose of showing affection. Kissing and touching are not necessarily associated with exploitation or lust, but they can be used that way.

A kiss or a touch of the hand should be a sign of special affection. If someone bestows these signs upon every boy or girl who comes around, they will not mean much. Save displays of affection for one special person; then these signs of endearment will be meaningful.

The word for "lust" is ἐπιθυμία (*epithumia*). A man has reached the brink of lust when he allows himself to become emotionally and physically aroused. When he uses signs of affection no longer to bestow affection, but for a means of gratifying desires in his body that he has no right to satisfy, that is when it is wrong. When a person becomes caught up in physical contact and allows it to evolve from affection to exploitation, that is no longer love; it is lust. When we test ourselves to see how far we can go without going too far, that is lust. That is a sin. Our Lord says to abstain.

Principles and Guidelines

Let me present some principles and guidelines to follow. I want to suggest that you need a good, healthy respect for your body. I really believe many young people get into trouble because they do not have this respect for their bodies. Paul wrote about this in 1 Corinthians 6:15–18:

> Do you not know that your bodies are members of Christ? Shall I then take away the members of Christ and make them members of a prostitute? May it never be! Or do you not know that the one who joins himself to a prostitute is one body with her? For He says, "The two shall become one flesh." But the one who joins himself to the Lord is one spirit with Him. Flee immorality. Every other sin that a man commits is outside the body, but the immoral man sins against his own body.

Paul said in a unique way that fornication is a violation against one's own body, one's person. It is not just a joining of two warm bodies. It is the joining of two souls, two spirits. It is the fusion of two personalities in a relationship that is to promote the greatest intimacy.

Paul talked of how unthinkable it would be to abuse a temple of the Holy Spirit like that:

> Or do you not know that your body is a temple of the Holy Spirit who is in you, whom you have from God, and that you are not your own? For you have been bought with a price: therefore glorify God in your body (1 Corinthians 6:19, 20).

We are children of God. That affects us not only spiritually and mentally, but also physically. We belong—heart, soul, and body—to Him. Certainly, that should impact our relationships with other people. More than anything else, the kind of person you are determines the kind of person you will marry. Good boys are looking for good girls, and good girls are looking for good boys. The right kind of person attracts the right kind. How careful you should be about your reputation!

Questions

1. What different interpretations or viewpoints exist for the Song of Solomon?

2. What problems have developed because people have not followed God's law concerning marriage?

3. What is one of the causes of trouble in premarital pitfalls?

4. What did Paul say concerning our bodies and the temple of the Holy Spirit (1 Corinthians 6:19)?

8
The Two Shall Become One

> *"It was said, 'Whoever sends his wife away, let him give her a certificate of divorce'; but I say to you that everyone who divorces his wife, except for the reason of unchastity, makes her commit adultery; and whoever marries a divorced woman commits adultery"* (Matthew 5:31, 32).

As I was preparing for this lesson, I looked back in my files for some past sermons on divorce and remarriage, and one of them said that in the United States, one thousand divorces were taking place every day. In a revision of that lesson, I found some updated statistics: 1,318 divorces per day. In years past, it was said that 1 out of every 3 marriages ended in divorce, and then it became 2 out of every 5. Now, perhaps 1 out of every 2 marriages ends in divorce. People have a flippant attitude in the world today toward marriage and divorce. Many have the idea that they will get married and, if it works out, that's fine—and if it doesn't work out, that's fine. They seem to think it does not matter.

I want us to look at what the Word of God has to say on the subject of marriage. I know that some of you may be thinking about getting married. Some of you may even be planning a marriage. I want to offer you some help for your marriage that is based on the Bible. As I see it, you and I can avoid the danger of divorce by doing two main things. We ought to live as God has commanded regarding marriage. We should also study and understand Jesus' teaching about divorce.

Conforming to God's Will: Marriage Is for Life

The first one of these is to make our lives conform to the will of God on the matter of marriage. In the very beginning, God created a man and a woman, and He planned that those two—and those two alone—should share their lives for as long as they both would live. In Genesis 2, God said, "It is not good for the man to be alone; I will make him a helper suitable for him" (2:18). "Suitable" means "answering to," "fitting to," or "corresponding to."

"So the Lord God caused a deep sleep to fall upon the man, and he slept; then He took one of his ribs..." (2:21). From this rib, God made a woman; and He "brought her to the man. The man said, 'This is now bone of my bones, and flesh of my flesh; she shall be called Woman, because she was taken out of Man'" (2:22, 23). Perhaps the author, Moses, added the next statement: "For this reason a man shall leave his father and mother and be joined to his wife; and they shall become one flesh" (2:24).

When God created man, He instituted marriage in this manner, and He intended that it be that way for all time. In Matthew 19:3, "some Pharisees came to Jesus, testing Him and asking, 'Is it lawful for a man to divorce his wife for any reason at all?'" Our Lord referred them to the very same passage I just called to your attention, Genesis 2.

> And He answered and said, "Have you not read that [God] who created them from the beginning made them male and female, and said, 'For this reason a man shall leave his father and mother and be joined to his wife, and the two shall become one flesh'? So they are no longer two, but one flesh. What therefore God has joined together, let no man separate" (Matthew 19:4–6).

Our Lord ratified the law that God had given at the beginning, the law that marriage is for life as long as both shall live. The union of marriage is of such an intimate nature that the two people are no longer two, but one. The very fact that woman was made from man shows that the two belong together. I am sure you have heard in sermons many times how woman's being taken from man's side shows that she was to be his companion and nearest to his heart. Matthew Henry wrote,

> . . . the woman was . . . not made out of his head to rule over him, nor out of his feet to be trampled upon by him, but out of his side to be equal with him, under his arm to be protected, and near his heart to be beloved.[1]

UNDERSTANDING JESUS' TEACHING ABOUT DIVORCE

Avoiding Departure from God's Plan

When sin came into the world, however, people began to depart from God's plan. For a while, God may even have tolerated this. The first bigamist we know of is Lamech. He is listed among the descendants of Cain. He had two wives, Adah and Zillah. The Bible also tells of a murder Lamech had committed. I think this is just part of showing the degenerative nature of Cain's line. Later, even men of God deviated from God's pattern for marriage.

For example, Abraham and Jacob both had a plurality of wives. Abraham had Sarah, who was unable to bear children; so Hagar bore a child for him. Jacob had two wives, Leah and Rachel. When Rachel was unable to bear children, Jacob had

---

[1]Matthew Henry, *Commentary on the Whole Bible: New One Volume Edition* (Grand Rapids, Mich.: Zondervan Publishing Co., 1961), 7.

children by Rachel's handmaid, Bilhah. Leah, seeing what Rachel had done, decided she could do the same thing; so she gave Zilpah to Jacob, and he had more children by her. All of these things were deviations from God's plan, but it became customary in those days.

Some documents found in Mesopotamia have been dated to about the time of Jacob. They tell that, in those days, if a woman was unable to have a child, it was customary for this woman to provide a handmaid who could bear her husband a child.

Most women today would not tolerate that, but it was customary then. In the days of David and Solomon, polygamy was rampant. Solomon had seven hundred wives and three hundred concubines. I doubt if anybody ever had more wives than that. Obviously, people were parting drastically from God's plan.

Examining Moses' Teaching on Divorce

It seems that even when the law of Moses was given, God made provisions. Returning to Matthew 19:7, we see that the Pharisees asked Jesus, after He had given His ruling on marriage, "Why then did Moses command to give her a certificate of divorce and send her away?" They were alluding to Deuteronomy 24:1–4, where Moses said,

> When a man takes a wife and marries her, and it happens that she finds no favor in his eyes because he has found some indecency in her, and he writes her a certificate of divorce and puts it in her hand and sends her out from his house, and she leaves his house and goes and becomes another man's wife, and if the latter husband turns against her and writes her a certificate of divorce and puts it in her hand and sends her out of his house, or if the latter husband dies who took her to be his wife, then her former husband who sent her away is not

allowed to take her again to be his wife, since she has been defiled; for that is an abomination before the LORD. . . .

Moses said, in other words, that a man could put away his wife, as long as he gave her a certificate of divorce. If she married another husband, though, the first one could not take her back, regardless of what happened. That was the ruling in Deuteronomy 24.

Our Lord said in Matthew 19 that this exception was given because of their "hardness of heart" (19:8). Moses realized, and God did too, that the children of Israel were of such a nature that restricting them to the basic law of one wife would have been too much for them. They would probably have ended up practicing open adultery or polygamy. Marriage was regulated in this way.

Our Lord added this: "But from the beginning it has not been this way" (19:8). In the days of Jesus, there was an ongoing argument among the Jews as to what reasons for putting away a wife were valid. Two opposing schools of thought existed: one conservative and the other liberal. The conservatives were of the school of Shammai, a respected rabbi during the Intertestamental Period. A more liberal view was held by the rabbi Hillel and his followers. The school of Shammai said that fornication was the only valid reason for divorce. Jesus ratified the teaching of the school of Shammai.

The school of Hillel believed in granting divorces if a woman spoke disrespectfully of her in-laws in the presence of her husband, if she burned the bread, or if she was a poor cook. Another reason was being quarrelsome or troublesome. Also, a woman could be divorced for being unable to bear a child for ten years. The biggest disgrace of all for a woman was to be unable to bear children, for children were the greatest status symbol. Therefore, if a man was married to a woman for ten years and she did not bear children, then he could divorce her, according to the school of Hillel.

What Jesus said about divorce was exactly what the school of Shammai believed. That brings us to Matthew 5:31, 32:

> "It was said, 'Whoever sends his wife away, let him give her a certificate of divorce'; but I say to you that everyone who divorces his wife, except for the reason of unchastity, makes her commit adultery; and whoever marries a divorced woman commits adultery."

In the Word of God, I can see only two reasons for a person to give up his or her marriage partner and marry again. One is death, and the other is fornication. Another passage, Romans 7:2, 3, talks about this. Paul gave a general rule, and that rule states that one who is married is bound for life:

> For the married woman is bound by law to her husband while he is living; but if her husband dies, she is released from the law concerning the husband. So then, if while her husband is living she is joined to another man, she shall be called an adulteress; but if her husband dies, she is free from that law, so that she is not an adulteress though she is joined to another man.

Our Lord gave the one exception: "Everyone who divorces his wife, *except for the reason of unchastity*, makes her commit adultery" (Matthew 5:31; emphasis mine). Jesus even said this twice in Matthew. Once might not have been enough for some.

> He said to them, "Because of your hardness of heart Moses permitted you to divorce your wives; but from the beginning it has not been this way. And I say to you, whoever divorces his wife, except for immorality, and marries another woman commits adultery" (Matthew 19:8, 9).

That means you cannot divorce your wife because she eats crackers in bed. If she is a drunkard, you still cannot divorce her with the right to remarry. If she curses you, you still cannot divorce her. If she is a murderer, you cannot. You might want to move in that case. You might be afraid to stay with her, but the Lord says there is only one reason for divorce and no other: fornication.

Nowadays, two people can easily get pieces of paper saying that they have been divorced. All kinds of reasons are being given for divorce, but the Word of God says only one reason is valid. Our Lord said in Matthew 19:6, "What therefore God has joined together, let no man separate."

What God has joined together, man cannot separate. You may have a piece of paper that says you have the right to marry someone else; but as far as the Word of God is concerned, you are bound to that person until the bond has been dissolved in God's eyes. The state may give you whatever kind of divorce you want, but our Lord has laid down His law in the Scriptures. No matter what laws may be passed where you live, His laws still stand.

Some Additional Teaching About Divorce

1. I have heard an interesting case made about Matthew 19:9, the passage that says you shall not put away your wife except for the cause of "fornication" in the King James Version. The case is based on the difference between "fornication," which is a sin committed by an unmarried person, and "adultery," which is a sin committed by a married person. Some think that when a man puts away his wife for "fornication," that means he is divorcing her because he found out she was not a virgin when he married her.

According to some particular rabbis, the word "indecency" in Deuteronomy 24:1 meant the woman was not a virgin. This argument is not necessarily true because the term "fornication" is not always restricted to unmarried people. Either a married or an unmarried person can commit fornication, according to the correct definition of the Greek word for "fornication," which is πορνεία (*porneia*). (The word "pornography" comes from that term. Literally, it means "fornication writing.") This particular Greek word covers the whole spectrum of sexual deviation. "Fornication" (*porneia*) includes adultery, premarital sex, and homosexuality. Any number of sexual sins would all be subsumed under the category of *porneia*. Our Lord was saying that if your partner is guilty of this type of sexual unfaithfulness, then you have the right to separate yourself from that situation and marry again.

2. You may wonder why Matthew 19:9 does not say anything about a woman's putting away her husband. In those days, a woman could not initiate a divorce. The woman had no choice as to whom she would marry. Her father just said, "You are to marry this man I have chosen for you. This was arranged when you were two years old." She could do nothing about it.

After she got married, she had no right to ask for a divorce. I think the laws given by our Lord relate to both sexes today. The law is this: No man can put away his wife except for the reason of fornication; no woman can put away her husband except for fornication. I think this is understandable. When we get married, we promise ourselves to each other. We promise that we will keep ourselves to one another as long as we both shall live. When one person breaks that vow, that releases the other one from his or her obligation.

3. Some of you may be thinking about 1 Corinthians 7 and wondering, "Isn't there another excuse for divorce and remarriage?" I do not think so. Paul said in 1 Corinthians 7:13–15:

> And a woman who has an unbelieving husband, and he consents to live with her, she must not send her husband away. For the unbelieving husband is sanctified through his wife, and the unbelieving wife is sanctified through her believing husband;

for otherwise your children are unclean, but now they are holy. Yet if the unbelieving one leaves, let him leave; the brother or the sister is not under bondage in such cases, but God has called us to peace.

He was talking about a situation involving a believing wife and an unbelieving husband. He was saying, I suppose, that if the unbelieving husband found the situation intolerable, then the believer could let him leave. I think Paul was implying that, if you must leave the unbeliever in order to be faithful to the Lord, then you should leave the unbeliever and remain a faithful Christian. When he said that the woman was "not under bondage" in such a case, I think he meant that she was not obligated to live with the unbelieving husband. Paul was not giving the Christian woman the right to leave the unbeliever and then remarry.

Jesus said, "Everyone who divorces his wife, except for the reason of unchastity, makes her commit adultery; and whoever marries a divorced woman commits adultery" (Matthew 5:32). When He made that statement, He gave only one exception, and I do not see how it makes sense to claim that Paul was giving another reason which Jesus neglected to mention.

Jesus said there is just one reason for divorce. If our Lord said there is only one, then I believe there is only one. It looks to me as if 1 Corinthians 7 is not talking about divorce so much as it is talking about a separation without the right to remarry. If I am wrong, you might be safe to disagree with me; but if the other position is wrong, you might be in trouble.

4. Some of you would be disappointed if we did not spend some time on what happens when people get into big messes and then later discover they are not scripturally married. How can we straighten it all out? I always hope that people will not ask me how to get out of a big marriage mess.

One time, I was preaching in Louisiana, and a man and

his wife had just begun attending church services. He had recently been baptized, and we were all delighted. He said one Sunday morning, "I want to talk to you after the worship service." We went into the office, and he said, "I think you ought to know that this is my fourth wife." I do not really know what to say to a person like that.

My wife once tried to talk with a woman who had been an active member of the church but was no longer faithful. She, too, was in a marriage mix-up. My wife encouraged her to come back to the church; and she said, "Why should I? According to you, as long as I stay in this marriage, I am lost anyway." Of course, we could ask, "Who do you love more: this husband you should not have, or the Lord?" Remarriage is a difficult problem to discuss.

In the Old Testament, it was made clear that men who had no right to be married to certain women had to send them away. When the people of Israel came back from Babylonian captivity, as recorded in the Books of Ezra and Nehemiah, the prophets took extreme measures to make the Israelites put away their pagan wives and their children. They had to dissolve unscriptural marriages. Ezra 10, in about the last twenty-five verses, lists those who put away their foreign wives.

An example in the New Testament is the encounter John the Baptist had with Herod Antipas. When Herod Antipas married his brother Philip's wife, what did John say to him? He told him in Matthew 14:4, "It is not lawful for you to have her." John went to jail for saying that. He was beheaded over taking a stand for what was right, but he never retracted his statement that Herod Antipas had no right to be married to that woman.

Paul said in Romans 7:2, 3,

> For the married woman is bound by law to her husband while he is living; but if her husband dies, she is released from the law concerning the husband. So then, if while her husband is living

she is joined to another man, she shall be called an adulteress; but if her husband dies, she is free from the law, so that she is not an adulteress though she is joined to another man.

The more I read this passage, the more convinced I am that unscriptural marriages cannot continue. That is a harsh thing to say to people. I do not know all the answers. Do you understand what this says? You have no right to marry again unless your partner is guilty of fornication or has died.

I think an ounce of prevention is worth a pound of cure—or maybe ten pounds of cure, in this case. I do not think I could continue to live with a wife if I learned that she did not have a scriptural divorce from her first husband. It is easy for me to say that because my wife did not have a husband before me. It is easy to take a stand on this question when it doesn't affect us, to sit in judgment and say what ought to be done. I have counseled many people who were faced with this problem, and it is a difficult one.

What about repentance? Can someone really repent of an adulterous union if he or she is still living with the same person? Restitution should be made, should it not? True repentance requires a change in one's life.

Conclusion

You cannot follow God's plan for marriage and divorce by yourself. It takes two to follow that plan. The best way to safeguard against these problems is to marry a person whose life is in harmony with God's will and understanding.

Questions

1. How can we avoid the danger of divorce?

2. In Genesis 2:18, what does "a helper suitable" mean?

3. What fact shows that man and woman belong together (Genesis 2:21)?

4. What did the school of Shammai teach?

5. What did the school of Hillel teach?

6. What is the one exception for divorce Jesus gave (Matthew 5:31, 32)?

7. What interesting case has been made concerning the passage about divorce found in Matthew 19?

8. What do some say is another excuse for divorce and remarriage (1 Corinthians 7:13–15)?

9
Five Suggestions For Parents

Fathers, do not provoke your children to anger; but bring them up in the discipline and instruction of the Lord (Ephesians 6:4).

There is a story of a bachelor preacher who had a sermon entitled "Commandments for Parents." After he got married and had his first child, he changed it to "Suggestions for Parents." When the second child came along, he called his sermon "Hints for Parents." When the third child came, he threw his sermon away altogether. You will notice the title for this lesson refers to "Suggestions for Parents" and not "Commandments for Parents." Among other things, having children teaches one a great deal of humility. At any rate, some things we know and experience from the Word of God will help us to be better parents. Some of them are presented here.

SPEND TIME TOGETHER

One of the problems in homes today is that everyone is too busy. Many young women ignore the exhortation of Titus 2:4, 5 to be workers at home.

We do certain things at certain times in our lives. If we do not do them at that time, they will likely never be done. When we are young, it is time to get an education and to date. It is difficult to do it later. There is a time when we care for aging parents. If we do not do it then, there will never be another opportunity. There is also a time in life when we must give attention to rearing our children. That is the only chance we get. Solomon said in Proverbs 19:18a, "Discipline your son while there is hope." It seems that he was indicating that there would be a time when there would be no hope.

We can spend time with our children in many ways. One of these is by working with them. It is good for children to have responsibilities, and it is good for us as parents to share those responsibilities such as cleaning the house, mowing the yard, working in the garden, or performing dozens of other tasks that we might think of. We are not doing our children any favor when we do not want them to work "as hard as we had to work" and, therefore, require nothing of them.

We can provide opportunities for togetherness by playing with our children. The moments that you will remember with the most pleasure as you look back upon your association with your children will probably be those you spent playing with your children. It is also true that, when children grow older, their fondest memories of their parents often are of the opportunities they had to be with them and play together.

Worship can be an opportunity to spend time with our children. We need to make time to have devotionals in our home. We must make arrangements to take our children to church and let them share the hours of worship with us.

Keep Open the Lines Of Communication

I firmly believe that if we can keep the lines of communication open with our children, there will be good things that come out of it. Too many parents raise the complaint, "I am like a stranger to my children." Too many children complain, "My parents won't listen to me."

Young people will find someone to talk with, someone in whom they can confide. They will get their advice from some-

FIVE SUGGESTIONS FOR PARENTS

where. How wonderful it is when they find this help from their mothers and fathers! There are some things we can do to keep the lines of communication open.

Show an interest in them and in what they are saying. We need to open up these lines of communication when our children are young. We need to let them know that we have time to listen to their little stories, that what is going on in their minds is important to us because they are important to us. One of the greatest compliments we can pay our children is to give them our undivided attention.

Be truthful with them. If we expect our children to be truthful with us, we must treat them in the same way. They need to know that we are telling them the truth at all times. We need to be sparing with our promises. We should make only promises that we can keep. We cannot expect our children to learn truth and honesty when we do not exemplify truth and honesty for them.

Try not to overreact. Sometimes children are afraid to tell their parents matters of an intimate nature for fear that they will overreact. It is hard for us as parents not to overreact, since we are so emotionally involved with our children; but we need to create a relationship with our children so that they can feel free to tell us whatever is on their hearts—however shocking that may be.

Do not push or pry. We must let our children tell us in their own good time what they want to tell us. To force them may destroy the line of communication instead of opening it. We must respect their privacy, even when we are eager to know something about their lives. We need to let them decide when to tell us.

Keep their confidence. Our children need to know that they can tell us something and it will be kept in confidence. We need to be extremely careful about what we tell on our children, especially in their presence. It takes only a few times of betraying their confidence before they will quit telling us anything of a confidential nature.

Keep quiet and listen. It is easy for us parents to want to sermonize and lecture to our children, but we need to give them a chance to tell their story without any interruptions. Parents need to be good listeners.

Give Them a Stable Home Environment

In broken homes, children are the biggest losers. Children cannot help it, but they are crippled if they come from a broken home. Nearly always, children from a broken home are insecure; quite often, they are loaded with guilt, thinking the problems in their home are their own fault.

One of the greatest ways you can guarantee that you will have a happy child is to love your mate. Let the children see that Mother loves Daddy and Daddy loves Mother. Let them see the security in that relationship. Children learn how to treat their spouses by watching their mother and father. I am sure that you have noticed that most of the problems such as child abuse and incest are in homes where the parents were treated the same way when they were children.

We need to present a united front as parents. It is easy for children to detect a disagreement between the parents and play one against the other. The story of Rebekah and Isaac in their dealings with Jacob and Esau is a perfect illustration of this.

Be Positive and Encouraging

Do not be overly critical of your child. It is so easy, when our child brings home a grade of 98 percent, to look at the paper and say, "Why did you miss those two?" It is easy to overlook the 98 points they got right and focus on the two they got wrong.

It has been said that it takes at least ten compliments to

overcome one negative remark. When ten people offer us compliments and only one gives us a criticism, we nearly always remember the criticism over the compliments.

We need to guard against comparing our children with other children, especially with brothers and sisters. We need to refrain from criticizing our children before others. Disciplinary matters, even criticism, should be a private matter so that our children will not be embarrassed in front of their friends or brothers and sisters.

We need to guard against applying too much pressure on our children. Often, parents try to realize or relive a childhood ambition in their children. It is a well-known fact that the biggest problems at Little League ballparks are not the children, but the parents. Sometimes the best thing we can do is just sit back and enjoy them and let them make mistakes. Even if they are not the greatest ball players on the team, we can love them for the fact that they wanted to get out there and try.

We must avoid creating negative attitudes. Go easy on the guilt. One line which could be left out of most conversations with our children is "After all I have done for you. . . ." We need to guard against being sarcastic or satirical. Very little is accomplished by sarcasm.

We need to be unafraid of expressing affection. It is not a sign of weakness for daddies to love their children or even to cry with them. I have few regrets, but the regrets I do have were over the times I was not patient enough with our children. I was not tender enough and did not express to them the love that I should have.

Exercise Discipline

Notice in Ephesians 6:4 that the responsibility of bringing up our children in the nurture and admonition of the Lord was given to fathers. It is their responsibility to take the lead in seeing that their wives receive help and support in establishing and maintaining guidelines for their children.

Children need to learn respect for authority at home. If they do not learn that respect there, it does not take long for the teachers at school to see it. If children have no respect for authority at home, they probably will not have respect for the laws of the land or even the laws of God. Our responsibility as parents is to teach this respect for and obedience to authority.

The first rule of discipline is that it must stem from love. We can discipline to the extent that we love our children. If they are secure in our love for them, we can discipline them well without doing them any harm.

Discipline should be reasonable. Children should know why they are receiving the discipline and understand the fairness of it. Perhaps this is the thought behind the exhortation in Ephesians 6:4 and Colossians 3:21 not to provoke our children to wrath.

Discipline should be consistent. Limits are not always at the same place. Sometimes we let our children get away with a lot more than we do at other times. If we are wrong, we should not be afraid to admit it. It will not make our children think any less of us when we admit we are wrong.

We need to be careful not to "paint ourselves into a corner." Avoid ultimatums such as "If you do that again, I'll spank you." We may not want to spank the child if he does it again, and now we have committed ourselves.

Do not be afraid to say "no." I think that some parents are afraid of their children. They are afraid to cross them. They are afraid they might "warp their little personalities."

Persistent discipline gives our children security. They need to have boundaries and know where those boundaries are. The hardest part in training our children is in the discipline. It requires a great deal of self-confidence on the part of the parent to make rules and to stand by them even when it may be unpleasant at the time. It is hard for us as parents to stand our ground when it looks like the friends of our children are permitted to do things that we do not want our children to do or to go places that we do not want them to go. It is hard for us as parents to hold back money when we know it is not good for them, while at the same time realizing that their playmates or peers have more money and possessions than ours do.

Conclusion

A song in *Camelot* says that the way to handle a woman is to "love her, simply love her, merely love her."[1] I am convinced that the way to handle a child is to love him, simply love him, merely love him. Rearing children is not an easy job, but it is worth all the trouble. The important things in life do not come easy. Rearing Christian men and women is one example of this. A child is the greatest gift God can bestow upon a home and also the greatest responsibility. Let us, as Christian mothers and fathers, rise to the opportunity God has given us with our children.

Questions

1. How can the lines of communication between parents and children be kept open?

2. What do children learn from seeing their parents in a healthy, loving relationship?

3. What is the first rule of discipline, and what does it mean for parents?

4. How does healthy discipline benefit children?

5. Why is discipline the hardest part of training children?

---

[1] Alan Jay Lerner and Frederick Loewe, "How to Handle a Woman," copyright 1960, administered by Chappell & Co.

10
Five More Suggestions For Parents

"These words, which I am commanding you today, shall be on your heart" (Deuteronomy 6:6).

Plant a radish.
Get a radish.
Never any doubt.
That's why I love vegetables;
You know what you're about![1]

These are the words of a song that was popular a number of years ago. The writer went on to say that with children it is quite different; you do not know what you have gotten until it is too late. I think all of us parents can identify with this apprehension about how our children are going to turn out.

Really, we cannot force our children to grow, develop, or be what they ought to be. It is a lot like planting a garden—all we can do is plant the seeds and try to create the proper environment and hope for growth.

At a teacher appreciation banquet for teachers at the College church, the little children were asked to give tributes to their teachers. The thing that impressed me most was that nearly every one of them talked about how they were treated

---

[1] "Plant a Radish," from *The Fantasticks* (https://www.allmusicals.com/lyrics/fantasticksthe/plantaradish.htm; Internet, accessed 12 April, 2022).

by the teacher, and not any of them talked about what they were taught by the teacher.

I wonder if we parents might learn a lesson from this. Our children learn more by the way we treat them than by the lessons we try to teach them. Here are some further suggestions that might help us do a better job with our children.

TEACH THEM RESPONSIBILITY

Our goal as parents is to help our children develop into responsible men and women so they can get along without us. Sometimes it makes us parents insecure when we see that our children can get along without us. Parents of Harding students ask me, "Where did I go wrong?" Their children come to Harding and are so happy they do not seem to miss home. I reply to them that they have not gone wrong; they have done their job well. The child we need to worry about is the one who is not able to stand on his own when the time in life comes for him to do so.

We need to let our children do as much for themselves as they are able. When Paul said in 1 Corinthians 13:5 that love "does not seek its own," he might have been indicating that true love does not hold the other person too closely or stifle his initiative. It would destroy our children to give them too much responsibility too soon. It also produces cripples when we make all their decisions for them and fight all of their battles for them. We have to let our children drive the car even though we wonder if they or the car will ever come back in one piece. We have to let them go away to school. We have to let them take the bumps and knocks of life on the playground and on the ball field. We cannot run interference for them all their lives.

Our children need to realize that the best way for us to give them more freedom and responsibility is for them to use well the freedom they have. We gradually give them more and more responsibility until they are able to make it on their own.

Teach Them the Word of God

> These words, which I am commanding you today, shall be on your heart. You shall teach them diligently to your sons and shall talk of them when you sit in your house and when you walk by the way and when you lie down and when you rise up. You shall bind them as a sign on your hand and they shall be as frontals on your forehead. You shall write them on the doorposts of your house and on your gates (Deuteronomy 6:6–9).

Moses very forcefully instructed the people of his day to train their children well.

We cannot expect the Sunday school to do all the Bible teaching for our children. Responsibility rests upon us as parents. The Bible schools can help us, but basically it is our responsibility.

We need to have devotionals with our children. We must set aside time in the evening or whenever they can all come together to sing and pray together and read the Word to them. I remember when our son was very small. At bedtime, he would get the song books and Bible and tell us, "It is time for our *commotion.*" When the children were little, he was more correct than he knew. It was a commotion, but at least they knew that we were trying.

Our children need to hear us pray. They need to receive instruction from us on how they should pray. They need to see the importance that the Bible holds in our lives and be taught from it as long as they are with us.

Plan a Christian Education for Them

One of the greatest gifts we can bestow on any child is a Christian education. I firmly believe that our young people who attend college should plan to attend one of our Christian schools.

A Christian environment is valuable. Our children are greatly influenced by their peers. How important it is for them to have the right kind of influence from their peers, to go to school with Christian young men and women who are committed to the same principles that they are!

Bible teaching received at a Christian college is valuable. Most of our Christian colleges have daily Bible classes for our college freshmen. Such intensive Bible training is far greater than we usually get in our Sunday school programs in our churches.

Developing leadership talent in the church is valuable. More and more, our church leaders are products of our Christian colleges. Our preachers, Bible teachers, elders, and missionaries, to a large degree, are those who have attended our Christian colleges.

Making Christian friends is an advantage. Wherever young people go after they have graduated from a Christian college, they can find friends in the church whom they knew while they were in college. This meant a great deal to me when our son graduated from Harding and moved to Dallas. Upon attending a church there, he found dozens of young people whom he already knew, friends he had made when he was a student at Harding.

You may say, "Of course you are in favor of Christian colleges because you teach at one." Really, the reverse is true. I teach at a Christian college because I see its value. I saw what a Christian education did for me, and I believe it can be of the same value to hundreds and thousands of our young people.

TEACH THEM TO MARRY A CHRISTIAN

Around 80 to 85 percent of our young people who attend a Christian college and marry a Christian remain faithful to the church. Probably less than 20 percent of our young people

FIVE MORE SUGGESTIONS FOR PARENTS

who have not attended a Christian college and marry outside the church remain faithful. I read that a church in Miami, Oklahoma, printed statistical information on their young people who had married during the past twenty years:

> One hundred forty-three Christian young people in our own congregation have married during the past 20 years. Seventy-nine married non-Christians. Of these, 57 have left the church with 25 being divorced, 22 are still faithful, and 14 have converted their mates. Sixty-four married Christians, and of these 59 are still faithful to the Lord. Only 2 of these marriages ended in divorce.[2]

The second most important decision that one will ever make in this life is whom he or she will marry. This is second only to the decision to follow Christ. More often than not, the most important decision, to follow Christ, is greatly influenced by the choice of a marriage partner.

Children have no choice as to whether or not they will be brought up in a Christian home, but their parents can make that decision for them. The greatest thing that you girls can do for your children would be to marry a Christian boy and give them a Christian father. Likewise, the greatest thing you young men can do would be to marry a Christian girl and give your children a Christian mother.

We parents need to teach our children diligently on the importance of marrying a Christian. We need to surround them with every possible opportunity to know and to date Christian young people. They can find these at church services, at youth camps, and at Christian colleges. We cannot determine just whom our child will marry, but we can place that child around so many Christians that the odds are stacked in our favor.

---

[2] This information appeared in the *Four State Gospel News* (November 1977).

Be a Christian Example Before Them

Little children are great imitators of parents. What little girl has not dressed up in her mother's clothes, and what little boy has not played that he was Daddy going off to work?

Our children are quick to recognize inconsistencies between what we say to them and the way we live in front of them. The best way that we can show our children what they ought to be is to live it in front of them. Until they can see true and complete dedication to Christ in our lives, it is hard for us to instill the same in them.

Conclusion

When Hannah prayed to God for a child, she promised to give him back to the Lord. As you remember, Samuel was born; and when the child was weaned, she gave him to the Lord. To some extent, I believe all of us are in the position of Hannah. The Lord has given us children, and the one thing we need to do most of all is to train those children so that we can present them back to Him.

I could ask for no greater blessing than for our whole family to stand in heaven redeemed with the circle unbroken. I am sure you feel the same way. To that end, let us dedicate our lives and our commitment as Christian mothers and fathers.

Questions

1. How do children learn from their parents?

2. What is the goal of parents?

3. Why do children need to hear their parents pray and see the importance that the study of the Bible holds in

their parents' lives?

4. What are the two most important decisions we make in life?

5. Why is it important for parents to be consistent in what they say and how they live in front of their children?

11
A Tribute to Christian Fathers

"For I have chosen him, so that he may command his children and his household after him to keep the way of the LORD by doing righteousness and justice, so that the LORD may bring upon Abraham what He has spoken about him" (Genesis 18:19).

Fathers play a large part in the Old Testament. Some fathers, such as Jeroboam, Amram, and Ahab, were bad. An interesting category is made up of good men who were bad fathers. A good and godly man is not necessarily a good father. Lot is an example. He was a good man, but he took his children to Sodom—and then what happened to his daughters? (See Genesis 13:8—19:38.)

Eli was a godly man, a priest, and a judge; yet the Lord tore the priesthood away from him and his whole family because of his children. (See 1 Samuel 2:12, 22; 3:12–14.) Israel desired a king because the children of Samuel did not walk in their father's ways. We can add David to this list of bad fathers. He had problems with Amnon, Absalom, and maybe even Adonijah and Solomon.

On the other hand, we read about some good, godly fathers in the Bible. Noah is an example of a good, godly father. In obedience to God, Noah prepared an ark to provide for the saving of his wife and his three children, along with their wives. Though he preached for 120 years, he was unable to save anyone else in the world. Nevertheless, he saved his household.

We must include Abraham. I think one of the greatest

compliments ever paid to a father is what God said of Abraham in Genesis 18:19:

> For I have chosen him, so that he may command his children and his household after him to keep the way of the LORD by doing righteousness and justice, so that the LORD may bring upon Abraham what He has spoken about him.

Abraham's love for the Lord was even greater than the love he had for his son. I think that is what helped to make him a good father. No man is the kind of father he should be unless he loves God more than he loves his children.

In Mark 9, we see a very tender picture of a father. He had taken his son to the disciples for healing, but they were unable to help him. The Lord had just come down from the mount of transfiguration with Peter, James, and John when the father approached Jesus. He told about the grievous torment the boy had experienced because of the demon within him. The father said in 9:22, "But if You can do anything, take pity on us and help us!"

Notice that the father did not say "help him," but "help us." He identified closely with the boy. The Lord repeated what the father had said: "'If You can'?" In other words, it would not be a lack of power on Jesus' part that would keep the boy from being healed. All things are possible for Jesus; and He said, "All things are possible to him who believes" (9:23). I love the father's response: "I do believe; help my unbelief" (9:24). In other words, he was desperately praying, "God, give me the faith. I believe. Give me the faith that my child can be healed." The outcome of that prayer was that the child was healed.

Those of us who are Christian fathers stand in a long line of good men, don't we? I think that Christian fathers deserve honor. Fathers function in a variety of roles, and I want to mention some of them to you and pay tribute to our fathers for the good that they do in fulfilling each of these roles.

HEAD OF THE HOUSE

The first of these is the father's role as the head of the house and husband of the wife. Ephesians 5:22–24 says,

> Wives, be subject to your own husbands, as to the Lord. For the husband is the head of the wife, as Christ also is the head of the church, He Himself being the Savior of the body. But as the church is subject to Christ, so also the wives ought to be to their husbands in everything.

This type of leadership or predominance is not one that has to be commanded. Respect is demanded by the very type of person the father is. You will find this to be true in life: The ones who are insecure in their positions are the ones who domineer or bully their way around. Those who have a quiet, calm serenity about them, because they know who they are, earn the respect that is due them by their very presence and behavior.

As David fled from Jerusalem during the rebellion of his son Absalom, he encountered a dissenter named Shimei (2 Samuel 16:5–13). Later, as David returned to Jerusalem, Shimei fell down before the king and begged for forgiveness (19:19, 20). Abishai, one of David's soldiers, asked, "Should not Shimei be put to death for this, because he cursed the LORD's anointed?" (19:21). In 19:22, David replied in the negative: ". . . Should any man be put to death in Israel today? For do I not know that I am king over Israel today?" When he had the confidence to act as king, he did not have to show it by being brutal to other people, by being abusive, or even by asserting himself.

I see that quality in the leadership of a Christian father, one who loves his family even more than he loves himself. A good man can stand strong and even sometimes be there quietly in the background, and his children and his wife look to him and recognize him for his position. It is a great responsibility to be the head of a household. It is a responsibility to be accountable for your own life, your own soul, your own welfare, and spiritual, social, and emotional needs; but when a man becomes the head of a household, he assumes additional responsibility for other people. He has the position of being accountable, in part, for his wife and his children. It is a great responsibility, and we pay tribute to men who fulfill that responsibility as they should. They deserve honor and support for it.

When a man assumes the position of the head of a house, his actions have more far-reaching effects. When I was a youngster, nobody paid much attention whether or not I was in a bad mood. As a father, if I got upset, what I said seems magnified throughout the home. Sometimes the things I said were magnified beyond what I meant for them to be because of my position as a husband and a father.

All of us fathers must be cautious. Sometimes we do not realize how our actions and our attitudes are echoed by our children. A father has qualities that set the tone of the home. We, as fathers, have a great responsibility to teach our children and to set the proper tone in our homes. We want to be the kind of leaders who can set the right atmosphere for our families so they can be happy, grow, and truly serve God. We pay tribute to fathers who are that kind of men.

FATHER

Second, the head of the house is a father to his children. Paul wrote, "Fathers, do not provoke your children to anger, but bring them up in the discipline and instruction of the Lord" (Ephesians 6:4). Again, we fathers stand in a unique situation. Children will defend their fathers, no matter what kind of men they may be. Have you ever noticed that? To your children—

young children, at least—you are the greatest in the world; and nothing is beyond your ability. You can be anything, and they want to be everything that you are. This places a heavy responsibility upon you.

We fathers have a unique situation. Our children want us to be great; they want us to be all that they think we are. We stand before them in a very responsible position. You and I have a responsibility as fathers to demonstrate what a godly man is and how he lives. Our children want to be like us.

When I was six years old, I used the scissors to cut the top of my hair off the back of my head. Do you know why? I wanted a bald spot like my father's. I remember my mother running out the door and seeing me in the backyard after it had been done. I remember her panicking and getting upset. I remember going to the barber so he could work on it. I also remember my disappointment when my hair grew back and my father's did not.

Each one of you, I imagine, could tell a similar story of how you wanted to be like your father or a time when you looked upon him as the ultimate. Concerning our responsibility to our children, fathers have unique obligations. An important one is spending time with our families.

It is ironic that the period of our lives when our children and families need us the most is the very period when we need to be working the hardest to make money to provide for them. If we are ever to succeed or advance in a chosen profession, that is the time when we must do it. A period of tension exists there. I know that the quality of time is said to be more important than the quantity of time spent with our children, but I do not see how we can have much quality without quantity.

A father needs a measure of firmness with his children. The father, as a rule, has a bit more distance from the children than the mother does, since she may spend more of the day with them. She identifies with them so closely that it is sometimes good to have someone who can see the situation more impartially, or maybe just reinforce what the mother has said.

If the children have listened to their mother all day long, what the father says when he comes home from work may carry more weight.

I think that the father has a special position, and he should recognize that. At times in the lives of the children, he may not be as close to them as their mother is; but he plays a very important role in laying down rules and guidelines for the family to follow.

I see in a father the importance of gentleness. The father is strong and sometimes rough, yet a little child can learn gentleness and strength at the hand of his father. I think children may learn more about gentleness from their fathers than from their mothers. I think that what parents need to do for their children, besides saving their souls by teaching them God's will, is to help the children feel good about themselves.

Many fathers are critical of their children. Even in front of other people, they sometimes make their children look bad and feel bad. It is easy for fathers to seem impatient with their children's small hands and not realize that these little ones are doing the best they can to please them. I think it is important for us to encourage children, to praise them, to love them, to hold them, and to tell them that we are proud of them. Whatever they do to show us that they want us to be proud of them, we should acknowledge their efforts and be proud of them if we possibly can. I would like for us to hold them and let them learn tenderness and kindness.

PROVIDER

Third, I think we should pay tribute to the father as the family's provider. Generally, he works at a job to supply what the family needs. "But if anyone does not provide for his own, and especially for those of his household, he has denied the faith and is worse than an unbeliever," said Paul in 1 Timothy 5:8. "For children are not responsible to save up for their parents, but parents for their children" (2 Corinthians 12:14). Jesus said,

Or what man is there among you who, when his son asks for a loaf, will give him a stone? Or if he asks for a fish, he will not give him a snake, will he? If you then, being evil, know how to give good gifts to your children, how much more will your Father who is in heaven give what is good to those who ask Him! (Matthew 7:9–11).

In turbulent times, it is financially difficult to be a provider. It is difficult for us to give our families all the material things that they need and protect them from the uncertainty and want that is all around us. Men sometimes feel inadequate because they cannot provide as much as they would like to provide for their families. Many times, frustration and other problems develop. Fathers know that there is a limit to their income, and they realize they cannot give the family everything they may want. We ought to encourage our fathers and recognize the responsibilities and pressures they have.

SPIRITUAL LEADER

Fourth, fathers are spiritual leaders. "But as for me and my house, we will serve the LORD," said Joshua in Joshua 24:15. It is our responsibility as fathers to set down and enforce the guidelines for what our children will do and what they will not do, as to how they will dress and how they will behave. I would be embarrassed for our children to participate in some of the activities in which other young people engage. It is our job as fathers to see that this is not done. We have abdicated our responsibility in many respects.

It is my responsibility as a father to see that my family worships God regularly. It is my responsibility to see that we pray at home. It is my responsibility to make sure that we read the Word of God together, study it, and have devotionals in our home. It is not the church's responsibility to teach my children His Word, though they may help with that effort.

"These words, which I am commanding you today, shall be on your heart. You shall teach them diligently to your sons and shall talk of them when you sit in your house and when you walk by the way and when you lie down and when you rise up. You shall bind them as a sign on your hand and they shall be as frontals on your forehead. You shall write them on the doorposts of your house and on your gates" (Deuteronomy 6:6–9).

The responsibility to be the spiritual leader in the family is the father's. The mother should help, but the burden is on the father. He is the spiritual leader. Therefore, we pay honor to the father as the head of the house, the father of the children, the provider for the home, and the spiritual leader of the household.

How can fathers be honored? Mothers and children, support your husbands and fathers. Let them know that you respect and appreciate them. "Honor your father and mother (which is the first commandment with a promise)" (Ephesians 6:2). Children, you should pay honor to your father and to your mother. You need to obey them.

Most of the time, you know exactly why your mother and father are telling you what you are to do and not to do, but there may be times when you may not think it is necessary. You may not see the sense in it. You need to trust them. They have more wisdom than you do. They may be wrong once in a while. You might even be right at times, but you need to trust them and be cooperative with them. They were young once. You need to volunteer honor to them. You should love them.

The most touching story I've ever heard is one that was told by D. L. Moody. A man whose small son was dying from an incurable disease was talking with him. As he held his hand, he asked, "Son, you are not afraid to die, are you?" The son replied, "I hate to leave you, but when I die I'll go to heaven where Jesus lives." "Yes, my child," said the heartbroken father.

The glazed eyes of the dying child sparkled as he gripped his father's hand. With his last breath, he spoke these words: "When I get to heaven, the first thing I'll do is to walk right up to Jesus and tell Him I had the best father who ever lived."[1]

Conclusion

May God add His blessing to these words and to your lives. May the joy and reward of being a Christian father be yours on this earth, as well as in the world to come.

Questions

1. Because a man is good and godly, does that mean he will be a good father?

2. What was one of the greatest compliments given to a father in the Bible (Genesis 18:19)? To whom was it given?

3. What helped to make Abraham a good father?

4. What quality in a father is very important?

5. What are some of the responsibilities of fathers?

---

[1] Adapted from D. L. Moody, "The Contrast," *The Standard* (March 24, 1900): 929.

12
A Tribute to Christian Mothers

Her children rise up and bless her;
Her husband also, and he praises her, saying:
"Many daughters have done nobly,
But you excel them all."
(Proverbs 31:28, 29).

In Exodus 20, we find the listing of the Ten Commandments. The first four of these ten have to do with man's relationship with God, and the last six concern man's relationship with his fellow man. In this second category, the first one is "Honor your father and your mother" (Exodus 20:12).

Nine out of the Ten Commandments are repeated in some form in the New Testament, but I do not think any of them are emphasized more than this one. In Ephesians 6:1–3, Paul said,

> Children, obey your parents in the Lord, for this is right. Honor your father and mother (which is the first commandment with a promise), so that it may be well with you, and that you may live long on the earth.

When we gather on the Lord's day, the primary emphasis is our worship of the Lord. We celebrate His resurrection. However, nothing is wrong with noticing the great contributions and honoring all of the wonderful services of our Christian mothers. They are a vital and integral part of our body. I think we are fulfilling the Scriptures by paying tribute to them.

In Romans 13:7, we read, "Render to all what is due them . . . honor to whom honor."

I want to give you three reasons for us to honor our mothers. Of course, there are many others; but we will focus on these three.

SERVICE

We honor our mothers for service that often goes unpraised. As far as glamorous jobs are concerned, motherhood does not qualify very well. Some of us get dressed up and go off to work, but mothers do not usually get dressed up. It would not help much if they did get dressed up. After a day on the job, we may come home with a sense of accomplishment for all that we have done. Even if a mother has been at home with the children all day, it may look as if she has not accomplished anything.

I heard about a man who came into the house, and everything seemed to be in a total mess. He and his wife had several children. He asked, "Didn't you get anything done today?" She replied, "I got everything done three times."

An old saying describes it this way: "A man works from sun to sun. A woman's work is never done." Few external rewards seem to come from being a mother. Very seldom is a woman voted "Mother of the Year." That makes it easy for a mother to feel at times that she is trapped in a thankless job. Women may think that motherhood is really not the greatest calling they could be answering. Quite a contrast is seen between our view today and the way the Hebrew people looked upon the service of motherhood. The ambition of every young Hebrew girl was to be a mother.

The key as to whether or not a woman was a good wife in biblical days was not how much poetry or literature she knew or where she had traveled. The important thing was that she could bear sons. Pressure was put on Sarah, Rebekah, and Rachel to bear sons. Motherhood would give them their sense of worth and value.

In Genesis 30, Rachel cried out because she had nothing. Leah had four children, but she had none. She said to Jacob, "Give me children, or else I die" (30:1). The story of Hannah is told in 1 Samuel 1. Her rival wife, Peninnah, had children. Hannah went into the tabernacle and prayed, "Lord, if You would just give me a son. I would give him back to You. He would be Yours all the days of his life" (see 1:11). Being a mother was her great ambition.

I have been told that every Hebrew young woman cherished in her heart the hope that she might be the mother of the Messiah. That, above all else, was the ambition of most young Hebrew girls.

In Judges 5:7, Deborah said, "Until I arose, a mother in Israel." She could have been called "the wife of Lappidoth." She could have referred to herself as "a prophetess." She could have called herself "a judge." She was the only female judge, and what a mark of distinction that was! Of all the things she could have been called, the one thing that seems to have given her the most pride and honor was being "a mother in Israel."

I would like to recall this type of honor and aspiration for motherhood today. Nothing is wrong with having ambitions. It bothers me sometimes that so many of our young girls have ambitions beyond, or separate from, that of being a mother. Of course, I know that a college trains people for professional work, but I hope our young women who attend college do not lose sight of the fact that the greatest service they can offer to society and the most important thing they can be in life has nothing to do with becoming a corporate executive. Young ladies, the most important service you can render in the Lord's kingdom, and the greatest honor you can ever bring to your life, comes with being a mother.

I think it is good for you to have aspirations, but I hope you never lose sight of the importance of being a mother. Prepare and train for that. I believe there is no greater honor or service for any woman than to be a godly mother.

Paul said in 1 Timothy 5:14, "Therefore, I want younger widows to get married, bear children, keep house, and give the enemy no occasion for reproach." He said in Titus 2:3, 4, "Older women likewise are to... encourage the young women to love their husbands, to love their children." The honor in the Word of God is associated with being a mother. One of the greatest areas of service that any young girl could ever aspire to is that of motherhood.

Our Lord called the disciples together one time in Matthew 20, when they were bickering over who would be the greatest in the kingdom. He said, "You know that the rulers of the Gentiles lord it over them, and their great men exercise authority over them. It is not this way among you, but whoever wishes to become great among you shall be your servant" (20:25, 26).

SELFLESS LOVE

We honor our mothers for their unselfish love. The love of a mother is proverbial. The first person whose love you ever felt as a child was your mother's. She carried you within her body for nine months, and then for the next few months she was the one who held you and fed you. Hers were the first sounds and smells and touches that you recognized. Hers was the first expression of love that you knew, even before your consciousness developed.

The love of a mother is a comforting love because we know it will always be there. We seldom worry about whether or not our mothers love us. Sometimes we may wish they did not love us quite so much in certain ways. We may worry about whether or not a certain boy or girl loves us, whether or not our teachers like us, or whether or not the boss is pleased with us; but most of us never worry about the love of our mothers. That is a solid security that stays with us. It is something, I think, that gives us our self-worth and helps us have better mental health for the rest of our lives.

This is something an eight-year-old wrote about a mother: "A mother is a person who takes care of her kids and gets their meals. If she was not there when you got home from school, you would not know how to get your meals, and you wouldn't feel like eating them anyhow." Little children feel such a warmth and such a comfort from a mother's love that even when we get old, we still remember those feelings.

The Bible is full of examples of motherly love. I have said many times that the husband may be the head of the house, but the wife and mother is the heart. I think that mothers have a quality and a capability of loving that no one else can equal.

In Romans 13:8, right after Paul said to honor those to whom honor is due, he said, "Owe nothing to anyone except to love one another. . . ." That kind of honor is a debt that we can never repay to our mothers. We can tell them we love them. We can go see them every opportunity we have, and we can remember them on every special occasion. We can express our appreciation for them in hundreds of ways, but all of these together fall far short of really communicating to them what it means to love them. We honor them for their unselfish love.

GODLY EXAMPLE

One time, an editor of *London Magazine* was writing an article on Winston Churchill, and he was listing Churchill's teachers. He showed the list to him, and Churchill said, "You have omitted to mention the greatest of all my teachers: my mother."[1]

Not only did your mother teach you about love, but it was probably your mother who first taught you about God. More

---

[1] Winston Churchill, quoted in "Churchill's Greatest Teacher Omitted," *The Journal of Education* 124 (September 1941): 209.

than likely, it was on her knee that you learned your first Bible verse or song. You may have sat on her lap in your first Bible class because you were too scared for her to leave you in there by yourself.

All those times when you kicked and squirmed and disrupted worship services, it was probably your mother who had brought you there, who kept you there, and who taught you to sit up and listen and behave. All the lessons that we need on how to deal with other people, how to love God, how to be considerate, and how to live were taught to us by our mothers.

One of the greatest preachers in the early church was Timothy. Paul complimented him. In 2 Timothy 1:5, Paul said, "For I am mindful of the sincere faith within you, which first dwelt in your grandmother Lois and your mother Eunice, and I am sure that it is in you as well." It has been well said that "the hand that rocks the cradle is the hand that rules the world."[2] I think any greatness men and women can claim probably goes back to the influence of a godly mother and to a home that provided the right start.

Many great tributes have been made by great men regarding their mothers. You might find a few of them interesting. John Quincy Adams said, "All that I am my mother made me."[3] James A. Garfield's first act after being inaugurated President of the United States was to stoop and kiss his aged mother, who sat near him.[4] Napoleon wisely said, "Let France have good mothers, and she will have good sons."[5] Henry Ward Beecher once said, "The memory of my mother as one

---

[2]William Ross Wallace, "The Hand That Rules theWorld," cited in John Bartlett, *Familiar Quotations*, 16th ed., ed. Justin Kaplan (Boston: Little, Brown, and Co., 1992), 488.

[3]John Quincy Adams, quoted in Dozier C. Cade, *Mama Was My Teacher: Growing Up in a Small Southern Town* (Lincoln, Nebr.: iUniverse, 2004), 77.

[4]James A. Garfield; accessed July 17, 2019; https://www.senate.gov/artandhistory/art/common/slideshow/Inauguration_1881.htm#1.

[5]Napoleon Bonaparte, quoted in Cade, 77.

A TRIBUTE TO CHRISTIAN MOTHERS

sainted has exerted a singular influence on me."[6] My favorite is the statement from Abraham Lincoln, who said on one occasion, "All that I am, or hope to be, I owe to my angel mother—blessings on her memory!"[7]

I want you to look at the last few verses of Proverbs 31:

> Her children rise up and bless her;
> Her husband also, and he praises her, saying:
> "Many daughters have done nobly,
> But you excel them all."
> Charm is deceitful and beauty is vain,
> But a woman who fears the LORD, she shall be
>   praised.
> Give her the product of her hands,
> And let her works praise her in the gates
>   (31:28–31).

Think of the mother you have been blessed with, and I hope you will encourage her and hold up her hands. Let her know beyond a doubt how important she is, how much you appreciate her, and what she means to you. I believe that mothers, as much as any other single factor, are the future of the church. From our mothers come our leaders, our preachers, our Bible teachers, our elders and deacons, our personal workers, and our soul-winners. May we never ever forget that! We honor mothers for their service that goes unpraised, for their unselfish love, and for being godly examples.

---

[6]Henry Ward Beecher, quoted in William C. Beecher and Samuel Scoville, assisted by Mrs. Henry Ward Beecher, *A Biography of Rev. Henry Ward Beecher* (New York: Charles L. Webster & Co., 1888), 67.

[7]Abraham Lincoln, quoted in J. G. Holland, *The Life of Abraham Lincoln* (New York: Dodd, Mead & Co., 1887), 23.

QUESTIONS

1. How did the Hebrew people look upon the service of motherhood?

2. Why is a mother's love an especially comforting love?

3. The husband may be the head of the house, but who is the heart?

4. Who was one of the greatest preachers in the early church whose faith was first found in his mother and grandmother (2 Timothy 1:5)?

5. What does Proverbs 31:28–31 say?

13
Trust
In the Home

"But let your statement be, 'Yes, yes' or 'No, no'; anything beyond these is of evil" (Matthew 5:37).

Basic to any of our relationships, if they are to be more than superficial, is trust. Good relationships must be based on trust. We do not do business with people whom we do not trust. When we look for a lawyer, an investor, or a doctor, one of the main things we look for is someone we trust. When we are in trouble and we need someone to count on, be with us, and help us, he or she must be somebody we trust. When we look for spiritual leaders, we look for those we trust. Trust makes all the difference.

GOD IS TRUSTWORTHY

One of the main qualities that God emphasizes about Himself in the Bible is that you can trust Him. The Hebrew word translated "lovingkindness" or "mercy" is חֶסֶד (*chesed*). The term does not have those exact meanings. The basic meaning of the word is "covenant loyalty." Again and again in Psalms, we find references to the *chesed* of God. He can always be trusted. When He makes a covenant, He will be loyal to it. ". . . let God be found true, though every man be found a liar . . ." (Romans 3:4). "If we are faithless, He remains faithful, for He cannot deny Himself" (2 Timothy 2:13). He has said, "I will never desert you, nor will I ever forsake you" (Hebrews 13:5b).

One really important quality that we see in God is that He is trustworthy. He is *chesed*. He endures forever. I want to apply that attribute to the home. As I look at it, at least four pillars are required to build a godly home. The first one is trust. The second is sharing. The third is forgiveness, and the fourth is love. These are four basic principles that must be present in the home, as God would have it.

TRUST BETWEEN PARENTS AND CHILDREN

Trust applies to the relationship between parents and children. We, as parents, must work at building the trust, or meriting the trust, of our children. Our children need someone they can trust. It is important for us to say what we mean and mean what we say with our children. As a father, I learned to avoid making rash promises I could not keep by using the expression "We will see."

Once you make a promise, you must keep it. Are we willing to live up to our commitments? Do our children know that we mean what we say, say what we mean, and can be trusted? Do they know that we tell the truth? I do not think parents ever have a valid excuse for lying to their children. At times, we do not tell them all of the truth because they are not ready to hear all of the truth. Sometimes we cannot tell our children something, but I believe that we must be truthful with our children. They need to know that we tell them the truth.

Once my son looked at me as I was telling him something and said, "I can't believe that." I asked, "Have I ever lied to you?" He replied, "No." I assured him that what I was saying was the truth. I may have been fooled, but I do not think our children have ever lied to their mother and father. If we want our children to trust us, then we must honor the confidence they have in us. Many times, our children may not tell us what they would like to tell us because they are afraid we will not keep it confidential.

I heard a statement from a fellow one time who said, "I will tell you a lie; and then if you can keep that secret, I will tell you the truth." That has happened in a lot of circumstances. People test each other to see if they can be trusted. Certain information may seem very trivial to us as parents. We may think some of our children's comments are funny, or they may have done something we would like to tell others; but privacy can be extremely important to our children. The little relationships we laugh at between boys and girls in the second grade, which are meaningless to us, really matter to second graders. When they have told us things in confidence, they need to know that we will keep their confidence. We must not betray their trust.

Our children need to see in us the kind of people who are truthful with others around us. They should be able to observe this quality in the way we speak to our wives, in the things we tell our husbands and our neighbors, and in the words they hear us say in phone conversations. I think one of the most important attributes we can develop in our children is trust.

I heard a story about a little boy who was stuck up in a tree and could not get down. A passerby said to him, "If you will just drop down, I will catch you." The boy said, "No, thanks, but you could go get my daddy and let him catch me."

You and I, as mothers and fathers, have to be the kind of people our children can trust. They still will not always tell us what they need to tell us. They may sometimes have reasons like fear of punishment or peer pressure. Nevertheless, if we are ever to develop the type of relationship with them in which we have that kind of rapport, they must be able to trust us. We have to be trustworthy.

Another side of this is that we have to teach our children to be trustworthy. It is important for them to tell us the truth. One of the most serious misdemeanors they can commit is lying to their parents. If they lie to us, then they have put us out of reach in helping them. If they do not talk to us truthfully, then we cannot know what is going on in their lives. It is a great moment in life when we learn that our children can be trusted. Teenagers often talk to me, and they sometimes ask how they can get their parents to allow them more freedom. I tell them to live up to the trust and responsibility they have already been given by their parents.

I do not think most parents actually want to manage their children's lives. We would love for them to be able to make decisions on their own, but we are afraid to give them too much freedom and responsibility until we can trust them with what they already have. We need to build relationships with our children early in their lives and then work to build on that to guide them through the teen years and the years beyond. We must have trust.

When problems arise in homes, it is too late to start working on building trust. Just when it seems as if home life is going well, some crisis occurs. When you have built the strong foundation of trust between parent and child, it will weather a lot of stormy problems. When you have a strong foundation of trust between husband and wife, minor conflicts will not divide the two. We cannot wait until the storms come and then decide to be trustworthy people.

Trust Between Husbands and Wives

One more factor is the relationship between husbands and wives. Marriage relationships must be built on trust. Husbands and wives need to be trustworthy. Married couples cannot have a proper relationship if they cannot trust each other. Some homes are like that.

If we are to have the kind of home that pleases God, that home must be based upon trust between a husband and a wife. Before I got married, I was visiting a congregation in Kentucky, and one of the elders there was talking about his wife. He made a comment that has stuck in my mind. He said, "We have been married a long time, and I just don't think I could ever live with another woman because we have grown so accustomed to each other." Do you know what he meant by that? He meant that they had a comfortable relationship because they trusted each other. They had lived together as husband and wife for many years. They had reared a family together. Their children were grown and had moved out of their home. These two were comfortable with one another. They had learned to trust each other.

It is comfortable to be in a relationship in which we trust those within the home. It is comfortable to be with someone, like a wife or a husband, with whom we can share our most intimate thoughts and know they will never betray those things to other people. Our greatest intimacies and confidentialities are safeguarded by a trustworthy spouse. Only in that kind of relationship can we make ourselves as vulnerable to each other as we need to be to have a right relationship.

Any kind of commitment or love makes you vulnerable to someone. Everything you tell that person, everything you do in an intimate way, makes you vulnerable to being betrayed. You will stop sharing with someone you cannot trust. You will pull away. We need to let our spouses know that they can trust us. Whatever may happen, they must be able to trust us.

In Matthew 5:33–37, Jesus said,

> Again, you have heard that the ancients were told, "You shall not make false vows, but shall fulfill your vows to the Lord." But I say to you, make no oath at all, either by heaven, for it is the throne of God, or by the earth, for it is the footstool of His feet, or by Jerusalem, for it is the city of the great King. Nor shall you make an oath by your head, for you cannot make one hair white or black. But let your statement be, "Yes, yes" or "No, no"; anything beyond these is of evil.

We may like the idea of what it means to take a vow, and we sometimes like to discuss how or when we can swear. These things are important to talk about, but that is not the main point our Lord was making in that passage.

The Lord was saying that you need to be the kind of person who can say "Yes" or "No," and that is all that is necessary because people know they can trust you. Those who know you believe that whatever you say is the truth; you do not have to swear by anyone or anything. Some people could swear with one hand on the Bible, and you still would not be sure they were telling the truth. Other people are of such quality that if they say something, it is believed.

That is the way it must be in the home. That is the way a wife must show her husband she is trustworthy. The passage in Proverbs 31 of the worthy woman says, "An excellent wife, who can find? For her worth is far above jewels. The heart of her husband trusts in her . . ." (31:10, 11). The primary quality in a good wife is that the heart of her husband trusts in her.

I do not think that we have to tell everything we know on every subject to our wives or our husbands. I think we are allowed to have a private part of our lives which we can keep private. Some thoughts would be hurtful if we shared them and would do no good. Burdening the other partner in a marriage with thoughts like that would serve no useful purpose.

I knew a young man who was very upset by this one time. His wife felt burdened to tell him certain things, and he did not want to hear them. He thought it would be better for their relationship if he did not hear everything she was thinking. I believe he was right, but an intimacy must exist between a husband and a wife. No secrets should exist between the two of them. Neither one should have any hidden agenda; the home should have an atmosphere of openness, freedom to speak, willingness to listen, and trust.

Many years ago, I found this reprinted in a church bulletin in Kentucky:

Preserve sacredly the privacies of your own house, your married state, and your heart. Let no father or mother or sister or brother ever presume to come between you, or share the joys or sorrows that belong to you two alone. With mutual help build your quiet world, not allowing your dearest earthly friends to be the confidant of [all] that concerns your domestic peace. Let the moments of alienation, if they occur, be healed at once. Never, no, never, speak of it outside; but to each other confess, and all will come out right. Never let the morrow's sun still find you at variance. Renew and renew your vow. It will do you good; and thereby your minds will grow together, contented in that love which is stronger than death, and your will be truly one.[1]

In order to build any other relationship, husbands and wives need, first of all, to build a relationship of mutual trust. We live in a world with too many uncertainties, too many cheaters and liars. Every one of us needs a haven from that—a place where there is acceptance, where there is openness and forgiveness. That place for each of us needs to be at home. It is crucial that our husbands and wives can trust us to be faithful to them!

If a woman left her husband and married you, you could not trust her. You would be married to someone who had broken her vows and had abandoned her family. She would likely do the same thing to you if she got the opportunity. Of course, people can change; but you would always have that doubt lurking in the back of your mind.

Years ago, I was flying into a city for a meeting. The section on the plane had three seats. I was sitting next to the

---

[1] "To Husband and Wife"; reprinted from *National Magazine*, in *Western Christian Advocate* 80 (March 4, 1914): 13.

window, and a woman and a man were sitting beside me. I had never seen people behaving as they were in a public place. He was hugging her and kissing her hand. This went on the whole trip, until we finally arrived. When I got off the plane, the man got off too; but the woman did not. I could not keep from seeing that the man's wife and three children were waiting to greet him. I know I should not be judgmental, but I could not believe it. I thought, "You scoundrel."

I wonder how many men slip off their wedding rings when they get on a plane. I wonder how many people can be trusted outside their home environment. When they are subjected to the temptations of being away from home, I wonder if they can be trusted. Can you be trusted?

Being married to a wife whom you trust is wonderful and comfortable. You do not have to worry about where she is when you are away from home. If she is talking with some other man, you do not have to worry. You also know that she trusts you, and you know in your heart that you would never do anything to betray that trust.

Trust is an odd thing. You cannot build it overnight. You do not have it immediately. When my wife and I were in another country, I was trying to buy a plane ticket with a credit card. The man who was selling the tickets said, "I'm sorry. You must use cash." I said, "Trust me. I'm an elder in the church. I even teach Bible classes! I always pay my bills." It meant nothing to him. He had no reason to trust me. He had never seen me before. Trust is something you have to build. If I did something foolish today that caused my wife to distrust me, it might take me thirty more years to build her trust in me back to where it is now. Many of us are working on a long history of trust with our wives or with our husbands. It would take only one foolish moment to destroy that. Trust is something that we have to build and continue to work on—something that gets stronger and stronger throughout the years. It is something we need to keep.

Malachi 2:13, 14 says,

> "This is another thing you do: you cover the altar of the LORD with tears, with weeping and with groaning, because He no longer regards the offering or accepts it with favor from your hand. Yet you say, 'For what reason?' Because the LORD has been a witness between you and the wife of your youth, against whom you have dealt treacherously, though she is your companion and your wife by covenant."

God would not even look at the offerings presented to Him by the Israelites at this time. He would not accept their prayers. He wanted nothing from them. He turned a deaf ear to their pleas because they were not trustworthy. They had broken the covenant.

Breaking a covenant is a serious matter in the Bible. In Hebrew, it is not "making" a covenant; it is literally "cutting" a covenant. Sometimes it may refer to chiseling in stone. It is a serious matter.

I was speaking to an out-of-town congregation, and a young girl came to me after the service and wanted to talk. She had married a good-looking man who was athletic and handsome. He had almost been killed in a car wreck, and he was now a paraplegic with severe brain damage. She wanted to know if she had the right to divorce him. She said, "I have needs. I am young. What can I do?" Do you know what I said to her? "Nothing. You promised to love and care for him in sickness and in health, for better or for worse. You promised that you would never leave him. If you made a promise like that, you have to live up to that promise. You have to keep your vows." I believe that is true for each of us. We are committed as much as is humanly possible to love that person, to care for that person, to stay with that person, and to be faithful to the vow that was made.

Here is a sample of the vows that are generally taken in a marriage ceremony:

Do you take this woman whose hand you now hold to be your lawfully wedded wife, to have and to hold from this day forward, for better, for worse, for richer or poorer, in sickness and in health, to love and to cherish until death do you part?

[The groom says, "I do." Then the preacher turns to the bride.]

Do you take this man whose hand you now hold to be your lawfully wedded husband, to have and to hold from this day forward, for better, for worse, for richer or poorer, in sickness and in health, to love and to cherish until death do you part? [Sometimes we add this line: "and forsaking all others, keeping yourself holy unto him, as long as you both shall live?"]

[She says, "I do."]

Once you have said "I do" to vows such as these, you are committed to that trust. Let us pray that nothing in this world can cause you to betray it.

Questions

1. Name one of the main qualities God emphasizes about Himself in the Bible.

2. What are the four pillars of a home?

3. What do trustworthy parents teach their children?

4. What point was Jesus making in Matthew 5:33–37?

5. What is our haven from the world?

14
Forgiveness In the Home

"For if you forgive others for their transgressions, your heavenly Father will also forgive you. But if you do not forgive others, then your Father will not forgive your transgressions" (Matthew 6:14, 15).

If I were to ask, "What is the most important ingredient in a marriage or in a home?" what would you say? Until recently, I probably would have said "communication." Many times, I have said communication is the lifeblood of a relationship in the home or anywhere else. I have changed my mind. I want to talk about the most important ingredient in a home.

I am now convinced that the most important ingredient is forgiveness. Our Lord said that if we will be forgiving of others, then He will forgive us. He even taught His disciples to pray, "Forgive us our debts, as we also have forgiven our debtors" (Matthew 6:12). If we refuse to forgive others, then we will be in a sad predicament when we need to be forgiven, as we surely will. I want to talk about relationships, the home, and the importance of forgiveness.

FORGIVING OUR CHILDREN

First, many of us need to forgive our children. Where feelings run the deepest, hurt can cut the worst. The world is full of disappointed parents whose children have brought them shame, embarrassment, and even bitterness. It is easy for us to think, "Is that all we get in return for all that we gave to our children?" Sometimes it is difficult not to be bitter toward those who have hurt us, but we must forgive our children.

In the Bible, David is a classic example of this. His son Absalom killed his half-brother Amnon, and David banished him from the country. David could not forgive him. After three years, Absalom finally got permission to come back into the country; but David said, "Let him not see my face" (2 Samuel 14:24). For two more years, David would not even see his son.

When my wife and I were in Palestine, we stayed in Jerusalem for some of the time, and I remember that the main highway in Jerusalem had three tombs with spotlights on them. We could see those tombs every night. One was supposed to be the tomb of Zacharias, the father of John the Baptist; one was identified as the tomb of James, the brother of Jesus; the third one, the tour guide said, was the tomb of Absalom.

I was looking out the window of the bus at those spotlighted tombs, and I thought, "What a continual reminder of a father who would not forgive his son!" The spotlight shone on a memorial of a life that could have been saved, had the father been willing to forgive.

Another story in the Bible illustrates the opposite. It is usually called "The Prodigal Son." As a young man was returning home after embarrassing himself and his entire family, his father saw him from a distance. That father ran to him. He embraced and kissed his son and said to the servants,

> Quickly bring out the best robe and put it on him, and put a ring on his hand and sandals on his feet; and bring the fattened calf, kill it, and let us eat and celebrate; for this son of mine was dead and has come to life again; he was lost and has been found ... (Luke 15:22–24).

I was told long ago that a Native American heard this story and was told, "This is the story of 'The Prodigal Son.'"

After listening to the story, he replied, "You should not call that 'The Prodigal Son,' but 'Father Great-Heart.'" Really, the emphasis is not on the boy, but on the father—a loving, forgiving father.

Our children will go beyond our pleasure and may often do things we think they should not be doing. As they grow older, they will realize that. Even as they become adults, they need to know that we cannot condone wrongdoing. We should let them know exactly what we believe to be right. However, they should always know that, if they return to God, they also have a home to which they can return.

After working with young people for a number of years, I am convinced that many desperate young people are looking for a place to turn. I hope that our children realize that, no matter where they go or what happens, there is a place where they can turn for help and guidance. They can knock on our door, and we will open it. Some of us, as parents, will have to forgive our children.

Forgiving Our Parents

Second, some of us, as children, need to learn to forgive our parents. A counselor was talking to me a while back; and he said, "My work is so discouraging. It seems that the root of nearly every person's troubles goes back to problems in the home with their parents." No parents are perfect, and probably all of us could think of something to resent about the way we were reared; but we need to overcome that. We cannot spend our lives resenting our parents.

An older man talked to me in a place not too far from here. He said, "When my father died, I didn't shed a tear. I was at the funeral, but I never shed a tear. All my life, I despised my father. I despised him for the way he treated me and my mother and the other children." As he talked to me, the bitterness seemed to flow. Then he totally changed his tone and said, "You know, now that I'm older, I've made peace with that. As

I look back on it, I have decided that, given the circumstances, he probably did the best he could." I think you and I must reach that same realization.

Our parents seem bigger than life when we are little; they control our lives and are more influential than anything else in the world around us. Then, one day, we grow up and see that they are just people. They are people who have troubles, problems, and weaknesses that we could not understand and maybe never even knew about as children. They were ordinary people trying to live through each day. Given the circumstances, maybe they just did the best they could.

I am firmly convinced of this: The first step toward healing is to forgive. I doubt that the hurts so many of us harbor and struggle with will ever be healed or overcome successfully until we find in our hearts the ability to forgive.

Many of the tears at funerals are not tears of grief, but tears of guilt shed by people who should have sought reconciliation with the deceased long ago. As children, we must learn to forgive our parents.

FORGIVING OUR BROTHERS AND SISTERS

Third, we must learn to forgive our brothers and our sisters—not only in our biological families, but also in our spiritual family. It is tragic that so many families avoid spending time together because one member of the family is not speaking to another. How many families have been divided because of a dispute over an inheritance or because someone feels as if he or she has been mistreated? Is any difference or disagreement really worth upsetting the whole family? I don't think so.

I heard of two preachers in Texas who were the best of enemies all their lives. They lived and worked together in the same general area, and they fought each other the whole time. They attacked each other in their bulletins and in the pulpit and even on the radio.

Finally, one of them became terminally ill, and the other went to see him in the hospital. He begged his forgiveness. The two embraced and prayed together and made peace. How much happier and more productive their lives would have been if they had done that sooner! How much stronger would the church have been? How many more people could have been led to the Lord? How much more vital could the Lord's people have been in that area, if only these two had just found it in their hearts to settle their disputes before they did?

Earlier, I mentioned the story of "The Prodigal Son." Jesus' focus in telling that story was not on the lost son. The rest of the story tells about the older brother, and that is what Jesus was emphasizing in Luke 15. When the younger son returned home, there was rejoicing. The older brother came in from the field and heard it, and he called a servant and inquired as to the meaning of it. The servant said, "Your brother has come, and your father has killed the fattened calf because he has received him back safe and sound" (15:27).

The elder brother would not take part in the celebration. The father came out and entreated him to join the party; but the brother said,

> Look! For so many years I have been serving you and I have never neglected a command of yours; and yet you have never given me a young goat, so that I might celebrate with my friends; but when this son of yours came, who has devoured your wealth with prostitutes, you killed the fattened calf for him (15:29, 30).

Do you hear the peevishness in that? "You never even gave me a little goat, but you killed the calf for him!" The father said, "Son, you have always been with me, and all that is mine is yours" (15:31).

Notice that the servant told the older brother, "Your

brother has come [home]." The elder brother did not call him his "brother." In speaking to his father, he referred to him as "this son of yours . . . , who has devoured your wealth with prostitutes." The father repeated, "But . . . this brother of yours . . . has been found" (15:32).

They had a nice little celebration that day; they had a wonderful meal. It would probably have been a lot happier if there had not been an empty place at the table. One chair was not occupied; one plate was not being used. Maybe, through an open window or doorway, those celebrating the young man's return could look outside and see the other brother with his back to them, looking up toward the sky, sitting on a stump, or maybe just kicking the ground. How much happier the whole group would have been if that boy could have come in and loved his brother and welcomed him home! How much nicer the whole occasion would have been!

I think we do not realize how much sorrow and hurt we bring upon others by our unforgiving spirits. Those around us are affected by our attitudes, and nearly everyone would be much happier if we could find it in our hearts to forgive.

An excellent contrast in the Bible is found in Genesis 50. When Jacob died, the brothers of Joseph thought he would surely kill them now that their father was dead because they had sold him into Egypt. They said, "What if Joseph bears a grudge against us and pays us back in full for all the wrong which we did to him!" (50:15). They begged for his forgiveness and said, "Your father said to forgive us, please" (see 50:17).

Do you remember Joseph's response in 50:19–21?

> But Joseph said to them, "Do not be afraid, for am I in God's place? As for you, you meant evil against me, but God meant it for good in order to bring about this present result, to preserve many people alive. So therefore, do not be afraid; I will provide for you and your little ones." So he comforted them and spoke kindly to them.

That made such a difference, didn't it? Joseph could have had a vengeful, spiteful spirit and made them all miserable. Instead, he said, "Dwell in the land, and let me care for you." That is what they did. They enjoyed life together, and they flourished in the land of Egypt. It has been said that Joseph is the one person in the Old Testament who was most like Jesus. This story makes a good argument for that statement.

You and I, many of us, need to find it in our hearts to make peace, to extend forgiveness to our brothers and our sisters.

Forgiving Our Husbands and Wives

Fourth, we must forgive our husbands and our wives. A poet said,

> We flatter those we scarcely know,
> We please the fleeting guest;
> And deal full many a thoughtless blow,
> To those who love us best.[1]

As I said before, where feelings run the deepest, hurt can cut the worst. People we do not care about cannot hurt us the way we can be hurt by those with whom our hearts are bound.

When we marry, we tend to think we have married perfection. It does not take long to discover we have not. Those cute little habits turn out to be very irritating sometimes. Now and then, we may wonder what we were thinking when we entered into marriage. We come to the realization that the spouse is just a regular person. We are supposed to love people; and the wife has to love her husband, for better or for worse. The husband is to love his wife, no matter what happens. These people will make mistakes because they are

---

[1]Ella Wheeler Wilcox, "Life's Scars," in *The Best Loved Poems of the American People,* selected by Hazel Felleman (New York: Doubleday, 1936), 645.

human. We all make mistakes. Just as we have to go and ask forgiveness at times, our spouses will occasionally have to ask for our forgiveness.

A man came to talk to me because he was having a problem; his wife had been unfaithful to him. He said, "I can't find it in my heart to forgive that. What can I do? What should I do?" I said to him, "If you would like to show that wife of yours that you love her in a way that you could never do before, I've got the answer for you." Most of us want to show our spouses that we love them. I said, "In a very special way, she will always remember how much you love her if you forgive her and never mention this again as long as you live together."

That is better than any gift you could buy. Did you know that? Sometimes it is difficult to buy a gift for someone you love. One thing that we all need but cannot buy for ourselves is forgiveness. That has to be given to us by someone else.

Do you remember the woman who was caught in the act of adultery in John 8? All of her accusers left, and then we read,

> Straightening up, Jesus said to her, "Woman, where are they? Did no one condemn you?" She said, "No one, Lord." And Jesus said, "I do not condemn you, either. Go. From now on sin no more" (8:10, 11).

If our Lord forgave, should we do any less?

The prophet Hosea had a wife, Gomer, who was unfaithful to him. She went after a number of lovers. It seems that her life just went downward and downward, until finally she was auctioned off on the slave block. Hosea saw her there, and he could have thought to himself, "That is what she deserves. I don't owe her anything." He didn't. He bought her freedom with what he had and brought her home to be his wife once more (see Hosea 3:2, 3). He loved her and forgave her.

His experience paralleled the way God loved Israel and wanted His people to repent; but this was the real story of a man who loved his wife enough to buy her back after the embarrassment, shame, and hurt that she had caused him. He took her to be his wife once more, and he forgave her. Regardless of her actions, do you think that woman ever doubted that Hosea loved her? In a very special, meaningful, and dramatic way, he said to her, "I love you, and I always will." We can do that ourselves as husbands and wives. Not only can we, but we must. We need to forgive our spouses.

Forgiving Ourselves

I have talked about four of the more intimate relationships: children, parents, brothers and sisters, and spouses. We all have one more person we must forgive, and this is probably the hardest of all: We need to forgive ourselves. Many of us are less forgiving of ourselves than we are of anyone else.

Many people are still punishing themselves with guilt for mistakes they made years ago—mistakes which God has forgiven. When God forgives, He forgets. That does not mean He can never remember them, but He does not hold them against us. We need to forgive ourselves and forget the past. If you are now a faithful Christian, then you must realize that the blood of Jesus has taken away all of your past sins.

Many of you have failed as husbands and wives. Some of you have gone through divorces, and some of you feel that you bear a lot of the blame for that. I doubt if there ever is a totally innocent party in a relationship. That is for God to judge, not me. What I am saying to you is that you have to forgive yourself. It is not the unpardonable sin that a marriage has failed; it is a bad thing, but it is not an unpardonable sin. You are not a second-class citizen in the kingdom of God; you do not have a mark on you in the church. You are forgiven! You need to forgive yourself and go on to be fruitful in the Lord's service.

You can do much for the Lord that no one else can do. You can minister to people whom the rest of us cannot serve as effectively as you can because of the experiences you have had.

A place for you is available in the kingdom of God; a place for you is waiting around the throne of God in heaven. You are God's child. You have been forgiven. It is time for you to forgive yourself and go on with the business of leading a productive Christian life, ministering and helping others.

Sometimes, as children, we have trouble forgiving ourselves for the way we treated our parents. Our parents may have died, and we never did tell them how much we loved them or ask for their forgiveness. If you could bring them back today, what would they tell you? I know what they would say to you. They would say, "Go on with your life. It's all right. Don't spend the rest of your life punishing yourself for that. Go forward and live as you should."

I believe that Proverbs 22:6 has probably laid more guilt upon parents than any other single verse. Some of us think that we have failed as parents. I know the anguish. I have listened as people talked to me about it, and I understand the helpless feeling of parents whose children are not living as they should. Almost immediately, the parents say, "Where did we go wrong?" I want to tell you that you may not have gone wrong.

Proverbs 22:6 says,

> Train up a child in the way he should go,
> Even when he is old he will not depart from it.

That is true as a general principle, and I think it proves itself in most cases. However, I do not believe we can use that to make a parent feel guilty. We cannot tell every parent with a child who has gone wrong, "You did a poor job as a parent. You have committed an unpardonable sin." Parents, you need to forgive yourselves, even if it is partly your fault that your child is leading an undisciplined life.

This is a proverb, and a proverb is a statement that is usually true but not 100 percent true. In the King James Version, Proverbs 26:4a says, "Answer not a fool according to his folly."

The next verse says, "Answer a fool according to his folly...."[2] This is true on one occasion but not on another. We have to understand the nature of a proverb when we read, "Train up a child in the way he should go." Training implies receptivity on the part of the child. It does not just say, "Teach."

Some animals are untrainable, and maybe some children are too. If it were true that every child who is trained in the way that he should go could never be unfaithful, then that would make the child predestined to be saved. That would take away his free will so that nothing he could do would cause him to be lost. Further, if this proverb were always true, this would be the only occasion I know of in which we would be held accountable for the results instead of our efforts. We are told to preach the gospel, but God will give the increase.

We should not feel guilty if someone we have taught does not accept the gospel. Children are ultimately responsible for the results of our teaching, but if the result does not turn out well, we tend to lay the guilt on the parents.

The converse of this is that some people grew up in horrible homes but became wonderful Christian men and women. The time comes when each individual person, regardless of his background, has to make decisions for himself or herself. I know that some of you came from less than ideal situations, yet you have become wonderful Christian men and women. Every human being has that choice and has that right. I think it is time to acknowledge the mistakes we have made in rearing our children and forgive ourselves for them. We cannot go about our lives in misery and guilt over our failures or presumed failures as parents.

I also think it is time for us to reach out our arms in love, kindness, and tenderness to forgive those against whom we have grudges. I heard Jimmy Allen[3] tell a story about a little

---

[2]The New American Standard Bible has "Answer a fool as his folly deserves" in 26:5a.

[3]Jimmy Allen (1930–2020) was a widely known evangelist who served as a Bible professor at Harding University in Searcy, Arkansas.

girl who was lost outdoors on one cold winter evening. People went out from the whole town, trying to find the little girl; but they were unable to do so. They knew that if they did not find her soon, she would freeze to death.

Finally, they decided that they would all start at one end of the large field where she had last been seen and walk across it, holding hands. They did, and they found the girl, but the little girl had died. It was too late. They were walking back to town quietly; and one was heard to say, "Would to God we had joined hands sooner." I would say to you, "May God guide us to join hands before it is too late, and find it in our hearts to forgive."

Questions

1. What is one of the most important ingredients in a marriage or in a home?

2. Whom do we need to forgive?

3. In a time of hurt, what is one of the first steps toward healing?

4. Since we all make mistakes, what will we have to do concerning our spouses?

5. The life of which prophet in the Old Testament paralleled the way God would deal with Israel?

6. What do we need to realize when we forgive ourselves?

Bibliography

Adams, John Quincy, quoted in Dozier C. Cade, *Mama Was My Teacher: Growing Up in a Small Southern Town* (Lincoln, Nebr.: iUniverse, 2004).

Beecher, Henry Ward, quoted in William C. Beecher and Samuel Scoville, assisted by Mrs. Henry Ward Beecher, *A Biography of Rev. Henry Ward Beecher* (New York: Charles L. Webster & Co., 1888).

Bonaparte, Napoleon, quoted in Dozier C. Cade, *Mama Was My Teacher: Growing Up in a Small Southern Town* (Lincoln, Nebr.: iUniverse, 2004).

Churchill, Winston, quoted in "Churchill's Greatest Teacher Omitted," *The Journal of Education* 124 (September 1941): 209.

Garfield, James A.; accessed July 17, 2019; https://www.senate.gov/artandhistory/art/common/slideshow/Inauguration_1881.htm#1.

Harvey, Paul. "What Are Fathers Made Of?"; accessed July 10, 2019; http://thisisrich.blogspot.com/2007/06/paul-harvey-what-are-fathers-made-of.html.

Henry, Matthew. *Commentary on the Whole Bible: New One Volume Edition* (Grand Rapids, Mich.: Zondervan Publishing Co., 1961).

Lerner, Alan Jay, and Frederick Loewe, "How to Handle a Woman," copyright 1960, administered by Chappell & Co.

Lincoln, Abraham, quoted in J. G. Holland, *The Life of Abraham Lincoln* (New York: Dodd, Mead & Co., 1887).

Moody, D. L. "The Contrast," *The Standard* (March 24, 1900): 929.

"To Husband and Wife"; reprinted from *National Magazine*, in *Western Christian Advocate* 80 (March 4, 1914): 13.

Wallace, William Ross. "The Hand That Rules the World," cited in John Bartlett, *Familiar Quotations*, 16th ed., ed. Justin Kaplan (Boston: Little, Brown, and Co., 1992).

Wilcox, Ella Wheeler. "Life's Scars," in *The Best Loved Poems of the American People*, selected by Hazel Felleman (New York: Doubleday, 1936).